According to the Scriptures?

Biblical Challenges in the Contemporary World

Editor: J. W. Rogerson, University of Sheffield

Current uses of the Bible in debates about issues such as human sexuality, war and wealth and poverty often amount to either a literalist concentration on a few selected texts, or an accommodation of the Bible to secular trends. The "Biblical Challenges" series aims to acquaint readers with the biblical material pertinent to particular issues, including that which causes difficulty or embarrassment in today's world, together with suggestions about how the Bible can nonetheless present a challenge in the contemporary age. The series seeks to open up a critical dialogue between the Bible and the chosen issue, which will lead to a dialogue between the biblical text and readers, challenging them to reflection and praxis. Each volume is designed with the needs of undergraduate and college students in mind, and can serve as a course book either for a complete unit or a component.

Forthcoming:

Fundamentalism and the Bible
Harriet A. Harris

The City in Biblical Perspective
John W. Rogerson and John Vincent

Science and Miracle, Faith and Doubt:
A Scientific Theology of the Bible
Mark Harris

According to the Scriptures?

The Challenge of Using the Bible in Social, Moral and Political Questions

J. W. Rogerson

London   Oakville

Published by

UK: Equinox Publishing Ltd., Unit 6, The Village, 101 Amies St., London SW11 2JW
USA: DBBC, 28 Main Street, Oakville, CT 06779

www.equinoxpub.com

First published 2007

© J. W. Rogerson 2007

British Library Cataloguing-in-Publication Data

A catalogue record for this book is available from the British Library.

ISBN-10   1 84553 127 2   (hardback)
           1 84553 128 0   (paperback)

ISBN-13   978 184553 127 0   (hardback)
           978 184553 128 7   (paperback)

Library of Congress Cataloging-in-Publication Data

Rogerson, J. W. (John William), 1935-
According to the Scriptures? : the challenge of using the Bible in
social, moral, and political questions / J.W. Rogerson.
    p. cm. -- (Biblical challenges in the contemporary world)
Includes bibliographical references and index.
ISBN-13: 978-1-84553-127-0 (hb)
ISBN-10: 1-84553-127-2 (hb)
ISBN-13: 978-1-84553-128-7 (pbk.)
ISBN-10: 1-84553-128-0 (pbk.)
1. Bible--Use. 2. Bible--Criticism, interpretation, etc. 3. Church
and social problems. I. Title. II. Series.
BS538.3.R68 2006
220.09--dc22
                        2006007944

Typeset by S.J.I. Services, New Delhi
Printed and bound in Great Britain by Lightning Source (UK) Ltd, Milton Keynes

For Rhianna,
in the hope that she will
read and enjoy this book,
and argue with me about its contents

CONTENTS

Preface

This book is intended as an introductory volume to a series entitled Biblical Challenges in the Contemporary World. Subsequent works on particular issues will be contributed by members of the Bible and Society Group, an informal and ecumenical group of biblical scholars who are committed to the Bible as a resource for thinking and acting on moral and social issues that confront today's world. While addressed primarily to members of churches who are also committed to the Bible as a foundation document of faith, it is to be hoped that the series will also be of interest to a general readership, and that it will indicate how the Bible can speak to today's world in a non-fundamentalist and non-literalist manner.

Among those whom I wish to thank are particularly the members of the Bible and Society Group, whose support and loyalty have been unwavering during years when it must have seemed that our deliberations would never yield any tangible results. We are especially grateful to Janet Joyce of Equinox for being willing to publish the series.

As ever, I am grateful to my wife Rosalind, who has word-processed the manuscript from my longhand. My niece Rhianna Fulford makes me very aware of the "real world" as experienced by a modern teenager, and she also has a lively interest in contemporary moral issues. I am happy to dedicate the book to her and await her reactions with considerable eagerness.

J. W. Rogerson
Sheffield
Candlemass, February 2006

Chapter 1

Can We "Go by the Book"?

Some years ago the Bible Societies in Britain ran a campaign to encourage more people to read the Bible, under the slogan "Go buy the book; go by the book." If we ignore the violence done to the English language in the first part, it has to be admitted that it is an eye-catching slogan. But what does it mean in practice? How does one "go by the book"?

Let us assume that someone has been persuaded by the slogan to buy a Bible, and that she begins to read it in order to discover what it means to "go by it" – to follow its commands. Because most people (except those who look first at the *last* pages of a detective story) open a book at the beginning, our reader starts with the first chapter of Genesis. The first commandment to the human race that she finds (Gen. 1:28) is to be fruitful and multiply. No doubt it made sense to have large families in a world in which many more children died in infancy than die similarly in today's affluent parts of the world. There was also the factor that war and disease made life expectancy much shorter in the ancient world than in the west today. But does the commandment make sense in today's over-populated world at the beginning of a century that will probably see even greater competition between nations for ever-diminishing natural resources such as water and oil?

The next command in Genesis (1:28) is to fill the earth, to subdue it and to have dominion over its other non-human inhabitants. The first part of the commandment, to fill the earth, has certainly been achieved; but it is arguable that the second and third parts have been so over-achieved that the human race ought to be diminishing the power it has to destroy rain forests and to drive many non-human species to extinction. Indeed, the ecological crisis facing today's world has been blamed on these verses (by White, 1967)!

In Genesis 1:29–30 our reader will find a passage that apparently envisages that humans will be vegetarians. Food for the human race will consist of "every plant yielding seed...and every tree with seed in its fruit."

If our reader is surprised by this and reads further on, she will find that Genesis 9:3–4 permits humans to eat the meat of animals, provided that it is prepared in such a way that the blood is first drained from it. This way of killing animals for food is practised today by Jews (kosher meat) and Moslems (halal meat) but not by Christians. If our reader reads further she will discover that not all animals may be consumed. Leviticus 11:2–23 and Deuteronomy 14:3–20 list animals whose meat may not be consumed. They include the hare and the pig. With regard to creatures that live in the water, only those with fins and scales are permitted, which presumably means that eels, crabs, lobsters, prawns and oysters are prohibited. If our reader looks almost to the end of the Bible, she will find that in Acts 10 Peter has a vision which apparently abolishes the distinction between clean (permitted) and unclean (prohibited) animals, and that Jesus is said at Mark 7:19 to have declared all foods to be clean (i.e., permitted for consumption). Our reader's researches will have uncovered the fact that "going by the book" is not simply a matter of reading a passage and obeying it. There may be other passages that modify it, as the permission to eat meat modifies the command to be vegetarian. The concession to eat meat may then first be restricted to certain types of meat, as in Leviticus 11 and so on; and may then be abolished altogether, as in Mark 7:19 and Acts 10. This will at least help our reader to understand why Jews (and Moslems) do not eat pork, while Christians do; but it will also be clear that some rules are needed about how passages are to be understood if one is going to "go by the book."

The next passage that our reader will meet is Genesis 2:2–3 which explains that God blessed and hallowed the seventh day, because he rested on this day, having completed the creation of the world. If we assume that our reader has read about the Sabbath day and that she follows up what she has read in Genesis 2:2–3, she will discover that the Sabbath day and the need to imitate God by resting upon it (i.e., doing no work) is a prominent theme in the Bible. The Ten Commandments in Exodus 20:2–17 and Deuteronomy 5:6–21 explicitly say that no work should be done on the Sabbath, and Exodus 20:11 justifies the commandment by referring back to Genesis 2:2–3. There are other passages that respect the injunction. Exodus 23:12 says that the Sabbath should be observed in order that the working domesticated animals and the slaves in a household should be allowed to rest for one day in seven. An earlier passage (Exod. 16:22–30) describes how the Israelites in the wilderness gathered twice as much manna on the sixth day than they did on previous days, so that they would not have to gather any on the Sabbath. At Numbers 15:32–36 a man is stoned to death because he was gathering sticks on the Sabbath day, presumably to light a fire. Jeremiah 17:19–27 condemns those who carry burdens in or out of their houses or the city of Jerusalem on the Sabbath day, while Nehemiah (governor of Jerusalem in the latter part of the fifth century BCE) takes measures to enforce the observance of the Sabbath (Neh. 13:19–22). In the New Testament, although Jesus comes into conflict with some of the religious teachers concerning whether it is lawful to heal on the Sabbath (Mark 3:1–6), he attends the synagogue worship on the Sabbath (Luke 4:16 – "he went to the synagogue, as his custom was, on the Sabbath day"). One of the surprising things about the Sabbath is that although it is such a prominent theme in the Bible, and there is no passage in the Bible that says that it has been abrogated, or superseded by Sunday, the almost overwhelming practice of Christians is to ignore the Bible's commandment about resting (i.e., doing no work) on the Sabbath (i.e., Friday evening to Saturday evening). Our reader will no doubt be curious to learn why, and upon what authority, such an apparently unambiguous command in the Bible has come to be so totally ignored, among Christians at any rate.

Genesis, chapters 2 and 3, contains material that has been used to teach male superiority over females. The man is created before the woman in Genesis 2:7 and indeed the woman is created from part of him to be a helper (Gen. 2:18). Following the disobedience of the first human couple, the woman is told that her husband will rule over her (Gen. 3:16). If our reader turns to the New Testament looking for an abrogation of these indications of male superiority, she will be disappointed. Ephesians 5:22 instructs wives to be subject to their husbands, while 1 Timothy 2:11–15, referring back to Genesis 3, declares that no woman is to teach or to have authority over men. Our reader does not have to be an ardent feminist to feel that such teaching hardly accords with the situation in the West today, where women work in all the professions in which men are active, including, in some Christian churches and also branches of Judaism, the exercise of priesthood, ministry, or the office of Rabbi. Does "going by the book" mean that such manifestations of female emancipation are contrary to God's will? This would certainly be the view of those churches that follow such an authoritative conservative work as Grudem (1994: 459–66). Yet the problem of the apparent counter-cultural demands of the Bible becomes particularly acute when the question of the death penalty is considered.

Genesis 9:6 states clearly that "whoever sheds the blood of man, by man shall his blood be shed." That is to say, the punishment for homicide, namely the intentional killing of another human being (other than in war, for the

Old Testament seems to take it for granted that killing in war is legitimate within certain limitations) is the judicial execution of the murderer. This is immediately problematic in today's world, for many nations, including those that were traditionally Christian in culture, have abolished the death penalty altogether. Great Britain, for example, as a signatory to the European Convention on Human Rights will not extradite a person to a country that retains the death penalty. Clearly, if there ever was a case of resisting cultural change by being faithful to the teaching of the Bible, it was on this issue; but the battle seems to have been lost. One does not hear "Bible-believing Christians" actively campaigning for the return of the death penalty in Britain, nor does one hear their leaders denouncing their country's apparent disregard for biblical teaching on this matter.

However, if our reader looks beyond Genesis 9 to Exodus 21, she will find that the death penalty is also required for the following offences:

- striking one's father or mother (Exod. 21:15)
- stealing a man (Exod. 21:16)
- cursing one's parents (Exod. 21:17).

In subsequent passages the death penalty is demanded for:

- being a sorceress (Exod. 22:18)
- having intercourse with an animal (Exod. 22:19)
- sacrificing to another god (Exod. 15:20)
- committing adultery (Lev. 20:10)
- various types of incest (Lev. 20:11–12)
- homosexual intercourse (Lev. 20:13)
- violating the Sabbath (Num. 15:32–36)
- inciting people to worship other gods (Deut. 13:1–18)
- being a stubborn and rebellious son (Deut. 21:18–21).

The point hardly needs to be made that anyone who maintained today that "going by the book" involved obedience to the regulations that prescribed the death penalty for these offences, would be regarded as insane. But this conclusion has implications for the earlier discussion about male superiority. If biblical commandments about enforcing the death penalty are either no longer appropriate to the modern world or are no longer enforceable, why should this not also be true of the Bible's teaching on male superiority? "Liberals" are often accused by "conservatives" in the churches of picking and choosing what they want from the Bible, whereas the "conservatives" are faithful to biblical teaching. But our reader might well ask why she should take notice of what the Bible says about male superiority when "Bible-believing Christians" clearly do not insist on the death penalty for adultery or cursing one's parents.

If our reader has not given up by now, she may reach Leviticus chapters 18 and 20 and may wonder what sort of families are implied by them. Leviticus 18:8–9 says that a man may not uncover the nakedness of (i.e., have intercourse with) his father's wife or the daughter of his father or the daughter of his mother. It seems odd to refer to one's mother and sister in this way, until it is realized that what is envisaged here is a polygamous family, that is, one in which a man has more than one wife. What is being prohibited is not intercourse between a man and his mother or sister, but intercourse between a man and one of his father's other wives, and between a man and the daughter that his father has had with another wife. Our reader will remember that various characters in the Old Testament have more than one wife, including Abraham (he fathers Ishmael by means of his wife's maid Hagar, Genesis 16:1–16), Jacob (who marries two sisters, Gen. 29:15–30), Samuel's father Elkanah (1 Sam. 1:2), David (1 Chron. 3:1–7 names seven wives), and Solomon (1 Kgs 11:3 mentions 700 wives and 300 concubines). These practices are clearly at variance with the laws of modern nations.

But Leviticus 18 and 20 became the basis for the rules formulated by the churches about who could marry whom. They laid down the close family relationships within which marriage was not permitted. Until the introduction of the Alternative Services in the Church of England in the late 1960s, generations of choirboys diverted their attention from boring sermons by reading the "Table of Kindred and Affinity" appended to the back of older printings of the Book of Common Prayer which listed those who were "forbidden in Scripture and in our laws to marry together." Among those listed was "Wife's sister," prohibiting a man from marrying the sister of his deceased wife. In the late-nineteenth century various attempts were made in the British parliament to abolish this particular prohibition, the attempt being opposed by the Church of England on the ground that the prohibition was part of the law of God. A supporter of the change was the playwright George Bernard Shaw, the plot of whose *Major Barbara* (1905) partly depended on the fact that marriage to the sister of one's deceased wife was legal in Australia but illegal in Britain. Thus, in the play, Adolphus Cusins, whose mother was the sister of her husband's first (deceased) wife, had been legitimately born from an Australian perspective but had been born out of wedlock according to British law. In 1907 the law was changed in Britain in spite of opposition from the Church of England. After the Second World War the Church also changed its rules to allow such marriages, and the "Table of Kindred and Affinity" was amended accordingly. What this example shows is that, in at least one particular, a national Church abandoned its attempt to uphold the "law of God" as derived from the Bible in the face of secular pressures, not to mention common sense.

Because our reader is blessed with particular stamina, she keeps reading until she gets to Deuteronomy 20:10, where she is frankly shocked by what she reads. She finds a passage saying that if the Israelites reach a city in time of war that will not accept the peace terms being offered to it, and in subsequent fighting defeat that city, then all the males in it are to be "put to the sword" (i.e., killed), while the women, children, cattle and other things found there, will be spoil for the Israelites. Our reader will surely be right to protest that such behaviour falls below even the dubious practices of supposedly civilized nations in the twentieth and twenty-first centuries, and that it is certainly in breach of various Geneva conventions. She will begin to wonder whether those who advised her to "go by the book" had ever read this far themselves, and how they would justify such injunctions as expressions of the will of God.

It is time to end this account of our reader's experiences of going through the first five books of the Bible, and to draw up a balance sheet. She has discovered the following things:

1. Some commands cannot be taken at face value because they may be expanded, modified or countermanded by other biblical passages. This was illustrated by the command to humanity to be vegetarian in Genesis 1:29, the modification allowing the consumption of meat in Genesis 9:3–4 and the question of which foods were permitted and which were prohibited.

2. Some commands appear to have been completely disregarded without any justification for this in the Bible itself. An example is the injunction to rest on the Sabbath day (i.e., from Friday evening to Saturday evening).

3. Some commandments could not be observed in today's world even if someone desired to do so. Cases in point would be the application of the death penalty to people who struck or cursed their parents, or who committed adultery, as well as the injunction to kill all the males of a conquered city and to take what remained of the population and possessions, as spoil.

4. There is a problem because some Christian groups hold that biblical teaching on male superiority is applicable in today's world, while

apparently not wanting to claim the same for the cases mentioned in paragraph 3 above. It is reasonable to want to know who decides what remains applicable and what ceases to be applicable, and on what grounds. A cynic could be forgiven for thinking that only those biblical commandments remain relevant that have not been declared illegal in modern nation states.

In the remainder of the book attempts will be made to deal with these, and other similar questions. The next chapter will consider Jewish insights into the matter, since the observance of commandments in the Hebrew Bible is at the heart of Judaism. Subsequent chapters will sketch the history of the use of the Bible in moral questions in the Christian churches, and the book will conclude with three specific case studies.

Chapter 2

"GOING BY THE BOOK": INSIGHTS FROM JUDAISM

Following the commandments of God as set down in the Bible is at the heart of Judaism. An observant Jew believes that God has graciously revealed his will to Israel, the people of God, so that his people can be assured in every detail of daily life that they are following God's commandments. However, it is not just the written Bible that is the source of this knowledge for Jews. The written law contained in the Bible is completed by an oral law, believed to have been revealed to Moses on Mount Sinai, and to have been passed down by word of mouth through many generations until it began to be set down in writing early in the Common Era. It is contained in the Mishnah, Tosephta, the Palestinian and Babylonian Talmuds, and its implications for modern living are drawn out from the principles contained in these writings as well as in the Bible.

It is not surprising that the Bible alone cannot be a complete guide to life in today's world. Its writers knew nothing of modern science, technology and travel, and the problems that are bound up with these things. Thus, road accidents or delays and cancellations in air travel or heart transplants, and ethical matters arising from them, could not be expected to be dealt with in the Bible. What is surprising, however, is that even within its own world and societies, the Bible contained nothing on a number of issues bound to affect any family. A good example is marriage. There are many references to marriage and people marrying, but no instructions as to how this should be done. Some passages hint at practices. The servant of Abraham who is sent to look for a wife for Isaac, gives Rebekah a ring for her nose and bracelets for her arms, presumably as pledges of his master's desire that Rebekah should marry Isaac (Gen. 24:15–49). The female speaker in the Song of Songs hints that her brothers have the power to decide whom she shall marry (Song 8:8–10). In Deuteronomy 25:1–10 the duty is placed upon a brother-in-law to marry his sister-in-law if she becomes a childless widow, and something like this practice is assumed in the book of Ruth where Ruth marries a relative of her mother-in-law. Again, there are hints in the book of Ruth and at Judges 21:20–23 that celebrations at harvest time were occasions when a certain amount of wooing took place. But there are no explicit rules about what happens when people get married. It is in the Mishnah tractate *Ketuvoth* (marriage contracts) that appropriate instructions are found.

Another good example is divorce. This is hinted at in Deuteronomy 24:1–4 from which it can be deduced that a ground for divorce is that a man finds "some indecency" (the exact meaning of this was a bone of contention in later Judaism) in his wife and that he writes her a bill of divorce. However, the purpose of the passage is to prohibit a man from remarrying a wife he has divorced and who has subsequently remarried and then become widowed or divorced. What the passage says about the mechanics of divorce is incidental, and one has to turn to the Mishnah tractate *Gittin* (bills of divorce) in order to get fuller details of divorce procedures. Adoption is another matter on which the Bible is silent, except for a hint at Genesis 15:3 where Abram may have adopted a slave, Eliezer, as his heir.

The fact that even within its own world and society the Hebrew Bible did not provide anything like comprehensive guidance on how to conduct daily life will make our presumed reader pause for thought. She will readily agree that an ancient text such as the Bible will hardly address problems that arise from modern science, technology and medicine; but she may be very surprised to discover that if she had lived at the time of and in the world of the Bible, she would have encountered numerous spheres of daily life in which she would not have been able to "go by the book" because the book was silent on these matters. In fact, the Bible was not alone in this regard. The same was true of other ancient collections of laws, such as the laws of Hammurabi, the king of Babylon, in the eighteenth century BCE. Although these were more extensive than the laws in the Bible they were by no means comprehensive. In fact, the comparative study of laws from the ancient world has made it clear that written collections of laws served to glorify the rulers under whose aegis they had been promulgated, rather than to enable law to be administered on a regular basis. The purpose of such collections was more ideological than legal and the same was true of the laws contained in the Bible. It has often been remarked that the collection known as the "Book of the Covenant" (the term is found in Exodus 24:7, and is a convenient way of describing the content of Exodus 21:1–23:19) begins with laws that limit slavery to six years, thus laying down the principle that among Israel, the people of God, slavery is not to be a permanent condition, even if it is an unfortunate social necessity for those who fall on hard times. Again, it has been pointed out that the laws of the Book of the Covenant evince a spirit of compassion for widows, orphans and the poor (Exod. 22:21–25), as well as for domesticated animals and household servants (Exod. 23:12). It has thus been argued that the purpose of the laws in the Hebrew Bible is to help express its theology – the implications at a practical level of belief in the God of Israel – rather than to lay down legal prescriptions; and to say this is to begin to admit a fundamental principle in the use of the Bible, namely, that the spirit that animates it is more important than the letter in which it is expressed. More will be said about this in later chapters.

The fact that Judaism was and is based upon the belief in two manifestations of God's law, one written (in the Bible) and one oral, did not, of course, diminish the importance of the written, biblical laws. However, their interpretation and application to ordinary life was not a simple matter, but one requiring a comprehensive knowledge of the biblical text and principles of interpretation. This will now be briefly illustrated with reference to one of the most important Jewish commentators, Rabbi Solomon ben Isaac (1040–1105 CE) who is usually know as Rashi, and who worked in Troyes, a town in northern France about 100 km from Paris.

Reference was made above (p. 4) to Exodus 21:15 which prescribes the death penalty for anyone who strikes his father or his mother. Rashi (see Rosenbaum and Silberman, 1946: 111–111a) notes that in other passages (Exod. 21:24–25) the Bible teaches that the infliction of a *wound* on another person incurs the penalty of damages, and concludes that in Exodus 21:15, the law says that anyone who inflicts a *wound* on a parent is subject to the death penalty. The issue is thus what is meant by "strikes," and the interpretation given by Rashi rules out any kind of blow that falls short of inflicting a wound. Two verses later the death penalty is prescribed for anyone who curses a parent. Rashi refers to a similar verse in Leviticus 20:9 which he takes to refer to a *man* cursing his parents and not a woman doing so. Since he believed that Exodus 21:17 refers to both men *and* women, he asks why there is a passage in Leviticus that appears to refer only to *men* who curse their parents. His conclusion is that the Leviticus passage is meant to refer to adults and to exclude minors.

The purpose of this illustration from Rashi is not to agree or disagree with his interpretation but to indicate the degree of sophistication involved in handling what, at first sight, look like straightforward commandments. "Going by the book" involves, in this and many other examples that could be brought from Rashi, a good deal more than a simplistic application of a commandment read literally.

Beyond the matter of how biblical commands are to be understood is the question of how they should be *applied*, especially in societies whose laws do not allow what the Bible commands. This can be illustrated by reference to the death penalty, which is the punishment prescribed in Exodus 21:15 and 17 for striking (wounding) or cursing one's parents. According to Jewish sources (cited in Safrai and Stern, 1974: 398–99) Jewish courts were denied the possibility of trying capital cases (i.e., those carrying the death penalty) for the period 30 to 70 CE, although this evidence is disputed. However, if the sources are correct, Judaism from at least the beginning of the Common Era had to adjust its practices in order to conform to the laws of the occupying power. One possible way in which this was done was by holding that a person guilty of a capital offence was punished, firstly, by misfortunes that would not otherwise have occurred and secondly, by a natural death that happened sooner than if the capital offence had not been carried out. Thirdly, the (premature) death of the guilty person exacted the penalty demanded by the Bible. The Day of Atonement could help to mitigate the guilt (see further Urbach, 1975: 431; [Hebrew 1971: 380–81]). With regard to the passage from Deuteronomy 20:10–18 concerning the killing of all males in a conquered city that did not accept peace terms, it is probable that this command belongs more to the rhetoric of war in the ancient world than to actual practice, although this is not to deny that its sentiments are disturbing to modern readers.

In today's world the demands of modern living create problems for observant Jews, especially in regard to keeping the Sabbath. Visitors to Jerusalem will be familiar with the way in which certain areas of the city are closed to motor vehicles on the Sabbath, in accordance with the view that the combustion of fuel in the engine of a motor vehicle breaks the Sabbath injunction about not kindling a flame. However, what is the position of a Jew living not in Jerusalem but a modern western city where the only way to get to a synagogue on the Sabbath is by driving or using public transport? This issue is discussed in a humane and sympathetic way by Novak (1974: 21–30) especially in the light of an opinion of three members of an American Conservative Jewish Rabbinical Assembly in 1950, that driving or riding to synagogue on the Sabbath could be legally justified. Novak takes a different view, but his discussion of the issues is a model of how one branch of modern Judaism deals with the application of biblical laws to modern situations. In fact, although Novak believes that a Jew who drives to synagogue on the Sabbath is violating it, he would regard the desire of the person concerned to come to the synagogue, as the opportunity to seek to persuade him or her to study the laws of Judaism more closely, with a view to honouring the Sabbath more appropriately.

The remainder of this book will be concerned with Christian attempts to interpret and apply the laws in the Bible to daily life. The purpose of this chapter on Jewish insights has been to note some aspects of the use of the Bible in a tradition that takes the observance of biblical commandments much more seriously than in Christianity. Even though the Christian understanding and use of the part of the Bible that is common to both faiths (i.e., the Hebrew Bible/Old Testament) has diverged considerably from Jewish understanding, there is much that Christians can learn from Jews in this area.

Chapter 3

THE OLD TESTAMENT LAW IN THE NEW TESTAMENT

There are two ways in which the interpretation and application of the Old Testament law in the New Testament can be approached. The first is to give a description of what is found in the New Testament read as a whole; the second is to use the New Testament as a source for reconstructing the development of the subject, from Jesus through Paul to the way in which the matter is presented in various New Testament writings. The first method has the advantage of being less controversial from the academic point of view, and of approaching the New Testament in the way that it was read for much of the history of the church until the rise of critical biblical scholarship. The second method touches on questions on which scholars are by no means agreed, and is circular in the sense that New Testament texts are critically evaluated in order that they might be interpreted. However, in spite of the problems involved, the second method will be followed because it brings into clearer light the reasons why, having emerged from Judaism, the early Church set itself on a course that diverged from Judaism so radically. The discussion by Luz (in Smend and Luz, 1981) will be the basis for what follows.

1. *Jesus*

If the attempt is made to disentangle the historical Jesus from how he is presented in the gospels, his ministry is best seen as determined by his conviction that the Kingdom of God has drawn near and that a new age is imminent. This new perspective brings with it a renewed demand for love among human beings, especially that one should love one's enemies. In fulfilment of this demand, Jesus associates with tax collectors and sinners and forms unconventional liaisons with groups of followers, which include women. His attitude to the Old Testament law is not one of hostility or opposition, or even of indifference; it is rather that his energies are concentrated in directions that leave little time or space for considering how the law should be applied.

The earliest followers of Jesus remained true to a commitment to the law as central to their faith. As Christianity spread in the non-Jewish world, however, the matter of adherence to the law, and to its outward symbol of circumcision, became an urgent question. Luz suggests (1981: 77) that the Jewish Christians had no difficulty in accepting converted Gentiles as though they were what Judaism called "God-fearers," that is, non-Jews who belonged to Jewish communities and who observed the commandments of the Jewish law without becoming circumcised. It was Paul and the Pauline churches that challenged this position.

2. *Paul*

Paul's attitude to the law was affected by his personal experience as an extremely sincere and zealous observer of the law, whose encounter with Christ had convinced him that his attempts to live according to the law were refuse (dung: Phil. 3:8). This was then grounded in theory in several ways. First, Paul referred to the passage in Deuteronomy 21:23, that a man whose body is hung upon a tree is accursed by God. In Deuteronomy the reference is to the body of someone who has committed a capital offence and has been executed, the body being displayed upon a tree, presumably as a warning to others. However, in Jewish texts of the beginning of the Common Era the verse was understood to refer to crucifixion. The Temple Scroll found among the Dead Sea Scrolls says (Column 64.9–11) "If a man has committed a capital offence…then you shall hang him on the wood, so that he dies. Yet they shall not let his corpse hang on the wood, but must bury it the same day, for cursed by God and men are those who are hanged on the wood" (see Maier, 1985: 55 and 132–34; [German 1978: 64 and 124–25]). Paul, according to Luz (1981: 91) argues that if God had raised from the dead one whose death was, according to the law, accursed, this amounted to a condemnation of the law itself.

Second, Paul argues in Romans 3:25–26 that the death of Christ had been an expiation for sin. This implies that the ritual laws of the Old Testament which prescribed various expiatory sacrifices had been rendered obsolete by Christ's death. Third, the idea of a New Covenant, which was embodied in the words used when the Lord's Supper was observed (1 Cor. 11:25), implied the passing of the Old Covenant, of which the Old Testament laws had been an integral part. Fourth, the expansion of Christianity in the non-Jewish world was seen as evidence that a new situation existed to which the Old Testament law, specific to Jews, was no longer applicable.

In fact, Luz calls these points the *presuppositions* of Paul's understanding of the law (Luz, 1981: 90) before describing in more detail Paul's particular wrestlings with the problem. His discussion can be briefly summarized under the following points:

1. Paul's personal experience of attempting to keep the law made it clear to him that such observance could not be the way of salvation.
2. His positive evaluation of the law was that it led to Christ.
3. Taking the word law in the wider sense of meaning the narratives of the Pentateuch, Paul's approach concentrated not upon its Mosaic, legislative material., but upon those parts that seemed to look forward to the promise of the gospel, for example, in the story of Abraham.
4. All the commands of the Old Testament could be summed up in the command to love one's neighbour (Rom. 13:8–10).
5. Paul did not regard himself as any longer subject to the Old Testament law.

3. The Gospels

This section will consider how Jesus is presented in the Gospels with regard to his attitude to the law, as opposed to what can be deduced from the Gospels about the position of the historical Jesus.

3.1. Matthew

In Matthew Jesus is described as affirming the law. His reference to it in the Sermon on the Mount ("you have heard it said...but I say unto you..." Matt. 5:21–22) are not denials of its authority or binding power, but declarations of Jesus' authority to give it a more profound meaning. According to Luz (1981: 79–86) Matthew's community was a Jewish Christian one in Syria, whose retention of the law was based upon the authority of Jesus, who was also seen to have fulfilled it. This is why in Matthew there is such emphasis on Christian *praxis* in the light of which people will be judged. However, this does not produce a righteousness of works. Obedience to God's commandments is a response to God's grace in making his will known and in offering salvation through Christ.

3.2. Mark

Mark gives a negative picture of Jesus' attitude to the law by emphasizing controversies with Jewish teachers concerning the Sabbath, and the matter of ritual purity. Luz thinks that the question of ritual purity was not one on which Jesus had pronounced, otherwise there would not have been so much disagreement about it in the early church (1981: 61). For example, would Peter have refused to eat with non-Jews (see Gal. 2:12) if Jesus had clearly taught that such table fellowship was permitted? Mark's presentation was probably shaped by the missionary situation of the church for which he wrote, one in which the presence of many non-Jewish converts acutely raised the question of ritual purity and observance of the Mosaic law.

3.3. *John*
John's gospel, too, has a negative picture of Jesus' attitude to the law, but it functions in a different way compared with Mark. In John, the controversies with Jewish teachers centre more than in Mark (but see Mark 2:10) upon the authority of Jesus as the Son of Man who comes in the Father's name. The Old Testament law (in its widest sense) bears witness to Jesus, and the failure of the Jews to see this is part of what condemns them. At the same time, John's Gospel affirms that observance of the Old Testament law is not the path to salvation. "The law was given through Moses; grace and truth came through Jesus Christ" (John 1:17).

4. *Luke and Acts*

These writings, according to Luz (1981: 131–34), presuppose a different situation from that of the other Gospels. The earlier generation of Jewish Christians has died out and the question of Christian identity is no longer an issue. Christians are not bound to the Jewish law (cp. Acts 15:1–29) and there is no suggestion that they should be. In this situation Luke portrays Jesus and indeed Paul (!) as observers of the Mosaic law; but that was at a time and place, which are now past. Indeed, the Lukan writings describe how the preaching of the gospel, which began in Jerusalem, spread to the further corners of the earth (cp. Acts 1:8), in the process bursting from its original Jewish setting to become a gospel for all peoples. The Old Testament law was no longer relevant or applicable in the missionary context of the Church's expansion among non-Jews. At the same time, the Old Testament remained the indispensable tool for understanding the universal mission and message of Jesus. On the Emmaus road, the risen Lord had interpreted what was written in Moses and the prophets in terms of his own sufferings and exaltation (Luke 24:27).

5. *Later New Testament Letters*

With the exception of the letter to the Hebrews, which sees the death of Christ as that which abolishes the sacrificial system of the Old Testament, the remaining New Testament letters are largely silent on the matter of the observance of the Old Testament laws. Their concern is much more to combat false teaching within the Christian communities. Even the letter of James, often considered to be an attempt to correct Paul's teaching on faith and works, shows no sign of finding problems with regard to the observance of the Old Testament laws. As with Paul, the writer of James has a broad approach to the Old Testament, citing examples not only from Abraham (James 2:21–24) but also from Rahab the harlot of Joshua 2:1–21 (James 2:25), Job (James 5:11) and Elijah (James 5:17–18). If, like Matthew's gospel, James lays stress upon praxis this is in the context of the "royal law" which sums up the practical injunctions of the Ten Commandment in the words "You shall love your neighbour as yourself" (James 2:8–12). The law that Christians are under is "the perfect law, the law of liberty" (James 1:25) which Luz (1981: 135) is inclined to identify as Jewish wisdom teaching shaped by memories of the teachings of Jesus.

Conclusions

This chapter has attempted the risky and controversial task of giving an historical sketch of how the churches of the New Testament era dealt with the matter of Christian observance of the Old Testament laws. It has done this in order to explain the next chapter, where an almost complete absence of reference to the Old Testament or its commandments is typical of the writings that are called the Apostolic Fathers and the Apologists. This absence is not so surprising in view of what this chapter has described. By the end of the first century CE, the churches had become separated from their Jewish roots and Christian congregations were made up largely of Gentiles. How Old Testament commandments should be regarded was not a central issue, although it would become an issue later in church history.

On the other hand, as was said earlier in the chapter, later users of the New Testament did not read it in the way that this chapter has done. As the issue of the Old Testament law became more prominent, later generations of theologians turned to the New Testament for guidance. Because different views about the Old Testament law could be found in the New Testament, ranging from Jesus' apparent endorsement of it in

Matthew and Luke, and his apparent rejection of it in Mark and John, not to mention the letters of Paul, scholars tended to find in the New Testament the answer that they were looking for. In modern times there has been a sharp division among New Testament experts regarding Paul's attitude to the law, depending on whether he is thought to have rejected it entirely or to have accepted it as the law of Christ. Underlying these divisions of opinion have been theological differences as between Lutherans and scholars in the Reformed tradition, traditions that have analysed the relationship between law and gospel in quite different ways. It will be the task of the next chapters to expand the history of how the Old Testament has been used, from New Testament times to the present day. This will be accompanied also by an account of how the New Testament was used in various, and differing, attempts to "go by the book."

Chapter 4

The Apostolic Fathers and Apologists

The survival of writings from the ancient world, especially those originally written on papyrus, is a matter of accident, and it is well known from references to them by authors, some of whose works did survive, that many ancient writings have been lost to posterity. Those that have not been lost are not necessarily representative of what was thought or practised generally, and this must be borne in mind when considering the so-called Apostolic Fathers, a name given to a number of texts written during the period approximately 95 to 159 CE. Yet when all allowance has been made for the possibility that these texts are not necessarily representative of what was believed and practised in the churches of that period, they show a remarkable similarity when it comes to the matter of the Old Testament law: they either generally ignore it, reject it or interpret it in a distinctively Christian way.

The earliest text, *1 Clement*, is full of quotations from the Old Testament, but these are directed towards the specific purpose of the letter, which was written by a leader (according to tradition, the bishop) of the church at Rome to the church at Corinth following the apparent ousting of established office holders in the Corinthian church by some younger members. The biblical examples are warnings against pride and jealousy and include the stories of Cain and Abel, Jacob and Esau, the flight of Moses from Pharaoh and the rebellion of Dathan and Abiram against Moses (*1 Clem.* 4). The letter also commends hospitality to strangers, citing the examples of Lot and the strangers who came to Sodom, and Rahab the harlot who welcomed the Israelite spies who came to Jericho (*1 Clem.* 11–12). When it comes to comments about the behaviour expected of Christians it is not to the Old Testament commandments that the writer turns, but to the psalms, and in particular, Psalm 50 (Ps. 49 in the ancient Greek translation; the writer of *1 Clement* knew the Bible in Greek, not Hebrew). It is true that Psalm 50 possibly refers to some of the Ten Commandments, and indeed *1 Clement* quotes the verses that seem to allude to them: "When you saw a thief, you ran together with him, and had fellowship with adulterers. Your mouth overflowed with wickedness and your tongue spoke deceitful things. You sat and spoke evil against your brother, and slandered your mother's son" (*1 Clem.* 35:8).

However, this quotation is preceded by a catalogue of evil doing that derives not from the Old Testament but, with variations, from Paul's letter to the Roman (1:28–32), itself a catalogue of evildoing popular in philosophical diatribes of the time. Also reminiscent of Paul is the statement in *1 Clement* 49:1 that whoever has love in Christ should keep the commandments of Christ, a statement that is followed by a praise of love which contains strong echoes of 1 Corinthians 13. The other positive ethical passage in *1 Clement* 38:2 stresses the duty of the strong and the rich to care for the weak and the poor, and the duty of the weak to respect the strong and of the poor to be thankful to God. Arguments based on silence are always problematic, but given that so much use is made in *1 Clement* of the Old Testament the lack of reference to its law or commandments is arguably not accidental.

The letters of Ignatius, bishop of Antioch, who was martyred in Rome early in the second century CE, are much more forthright in rejecting parts of the Old Testament law that Ignatius associates with Judaism. *Magnesians* 8:1 states that those who follow Jewish customs declare that they have not received the grace of Jesus Christ. The Old Testament prophets lived according to the teaching of Jesus (*Mag.* 8:2) and Christians, who live according to a new hope, no longer observe the Sabbath but the Lord's Day (*Mag.* 9:1). *Magnesians* 10:3 asserts that it is not appropriate to speak of Jesus Christ and to live according to Jewish customs, while *Philadelphians* 6:1 advises Christians not to listen to anyone who speaks about Judaism. It is better to hear about Christianity from a circumcised person than to hear about Judaism from someone uncircumcised. The context indicates that the references to Judaism include teaching about Jesus that includes or involves adherence to some Jewish customs.

The letters of Clement and Ignatius are occasional pieces, writings directed to particular circumstances and therefore only incidentally evidence for attitudes to Christian ethical practice. A work that comes much closer to being a compendium on Christian behaviour is the Shepherd of Hermas, written in Rome, probably in the first half of the second century CE, and bound up with the New Testament in the great fourth-century Codex Sinaiticus (although the latter part is missing). The Shepherd of Hermas contains a number of visions granted to the author, which include at one point the disclosure of twelve commandments. The surprising thing about them is that they contain no reference to the Ten Commandments or, indeed, to other Old Testament laws. Commandment four, for example, deals with divorce. The question discussed is whether a man should continue to live with his believing (Christian) wife if she commits adultery (Hermas, *Mand.* 4.4). The answer given is that if the husband is aware of the act and the woman persists in the adulterous relationship, then he should divorce her. He may not remarry, however, because he has a duty to take his former wife back if she repents and wishes to return to him. It is added that the same rules apply to both the husband and the wife (Hermas, *Mand.* 4.8). In what follows immediately afterwards, idolatrous worship is likened to adultery, and the rules about a husband leaving a wife or vice versa if one of the partners persists in the act, is repeated. It is noteworthy that the subject of divorce is dealt with without reference to any biblical passages, from either the Old Testament or the New. In the section containing commandment eight extensive lists of good and bad works are given. While several such as adultery, stealing, bearing false witness or, on the good side, supporting widows and orphans, can be paralleled from the Old Testament, the lists taken as a whole do not give the impression of being derived from the Bible. Rather, they are catalogues of good and bad deeds that would be approved by any moral teacher, put into a Christian context by the insistence that a servant (or slave) of God should avoid the one and practise the other. The Shepherd of Hermas seems to indicate that however the Christian community at Rome in the first half of the second century conceived its sources of moral authority these were not taken directly from the Bible.

The so-called *Letter of Barnabas*, often dated to around 130 CE, but whose place and occasion of composition are disputed, was also bound up with the New Testament part of Codex Sinaiticus. Its treatment of the Old Testament law is the most striking among the Apostolic Fathers. Its rejection of the system of Old Testament sacrifices is based not simply on the belief that Christ's sacrificial death has made these unnecessary, but rather on the view that they were not desired by God within the religion of Israel. A key text is Jeremiah 7:22 with its rhetorical question, "Did I command your fathers, when they came out of the land of Egypt, to bring me burnt offerings and sacrifices?" The author of *Barnabas* assumes that the answer was no, for he adds, "Instead of this I commanded that none of you should devise evil in your heart against your neighbour, nor love a false oath" (*Barn.* 2:7–8 quoting Jer. 7:22–23a and Zech. 8:17a). This is backed up by the critique of Israelite sacrifice in Isaiah 1:11–13 and by a text much used in the Apostolic Fathers, "a sacrifice for the Lord is a broken heart" (Ps.

51:17; Greek 50:19). Fasting is condemned on the basis of Isaiah 58:6–10, a highly rhetorical passage which defines the fast acceptable to God in terms of social justice and compassion. However, the most remarkable passage occurs at *Barnabas* 4:7–8 where it is argued that God's covenant (the Old Testament) is "ours," that is, it is with Christians because the Jews lost it when Moses destroyed the original tablets on which the Ten Commandments were written (cp. Deut. 9:17).

In what sense, then does the (Old) Covenant belong to Christians? It belongs to them in the sense that it should not be taken literally, but read in a spiritual way. Here follows the famous passage in which the prohibition against eating unclean animals is taken to mean that Christians should avoid fellowship with certain types of person (*Barn.* 10:1–8). The prohibition on eating pork alludes to avoiding contact with people of a pig-like disposition. Birds of prey indicate people who live not by honest labour but by lawlessness and theft. Hares indicate child molesters while the hyena, which changes its sex annually, warns against adultery and seduction. The treatment of the Sabbath law interprets a day as a thousand years, which means that God's purpose will be complete after 6,000 years. God's rest on the seventh day (Gen. 2:2) means that God will rest when his Son has come and has put an end to the time of lawlessness (*Barn.* 15:3–5). The Jewish Sabbath is further rejected by means of Isa. 1:13, "I cannot bear your new moons and Sabbaths" and in its place is the honouring of the eighth day, the day on which Jesus both rose from the dead and ascended to heaven (*Barn.* 15:9). Barnabas here exhibits the view, common in the early church, that resurrection and ascension occurred on the same (single) day.

The letter concludes with a description of the two ways, the way of light and the way of darkness. The virtues and vices listed are very similar to those in the description of the two ways in the *Didache* (of which more shortly), and indicate that this teaching was, if not widespread, at least not confined to one particular community. As in the case of the Shepherd of Hermas, while some of the commandments can be paralleled from passages in the Old Testament, the impression overall is that their source is not the Bible directly. An indication of this can be seen from the following extract from *Barnabas* 19:2–35: "Do not abandon the commandments of the Lord. You shall not exalt yourself but rather be humble in every way. You shall not seek honour for yourself. You shall not make any evil decision against your neighbour. You shall not be insolent. You shall not fornicate, not commit adultery, nor abuse children. Do not take the Lord's name in vain. You shall love your neighbour more than yourself. You shall not procure an abortion or abandon a new-born child." The description of the two ways ends with the command to learn and obey the injunctions of the Lord, as they are written. According to one commentator (Wengst, 1984: 193) this means that the author of Barnabas viewed the doctrine of the two ways as authoritative "Scripture." If this is correct it indicates that parts, at least, of the early Church had a much broader view of what constituted "Scripture" than was the case in later times, and that a broad view was taken of the sources for moral authority.

The text known as the *Didache* or the *Teaching of the Twelve Apostles*, thought to have been put together from various sources by its (unknown) author around 100 CE in Palestine or Syria (Rordorf, 1999: 836), begins with a description of the two ways between which Christians must choose. As in the case of the very similar, but not identical, material in *Barnabas*, the injunctions do not appear to be taken directly from the Bible, although certain of them can be paralleled from the Bible. Thus, *Didache* 2:2 begins by prohibiting murder and adultery, but then lists, in this order, molesting children, committing adultery, dealing with magic, mixing poisons, procuring an abortion, abandoning a newly-born child, coveting the possessions of one's neighbour, swearing a false oath, bearing false witness, speaking evil, and bearing malice. There follow warnings not to be deliberately ambiguous or double-tongued, while greed, robbery, hypocrisy, cunning and pride are forbidden. The injunction to hate no one is supplemented by the command to pray for many and to love some, more than one loves oneself. On the positive side deeds of kindness and the support of the poor are enjoined (*Did.* 4:8). An interesting passage is that dealing with slavery (*Did.* 4:10). Here masters are told not to behave towards their slaves, who are also believers, in such a way as to stop them from believing. God does not call people in virtue of their worldly position. On the other hand, slaves are to respect their masters as though the latter were a representation (Greek, *tupos*) of God. As in the case of Paul's remarks about slavery, there is no mention of the fact that Old Testament laws on slavery require the freedom of the slave after six years (Exod. 21:2; Deut. 15:12). The early Church seems to have accepted the rules that governed slavery generally in their society, and to have ignored the teaching of the Bible on this issue (see further Klein, 2000: 379).

The Apologists were Christian writers of the second and third centuries CE who defended Christianity against the representatives of the Roman Empire, against Jewish teachers, and against groups that claimed to be Christian but were adjudged to be heretical by the emerging "catholic" church. Obviously, their works were affected by the situations in which they were written; however, their essential continuity with the views found in the Apostolic Fathers on matters pertaining to the law and ethics is clear.

Justin Martyr, whose *Dialogue with Trypho* will be discussed here, was born in Flavia Neapolis (today's Nablus in Palestine) of pagan parents, and having studied philosophy, embraced Christianity with such conviction that he suffered martyrdom for his faith in 165 CE in Rome. His *Dialogue with Trypho*, a Jew, usually dated to 155–160 CE, contains a moving account of the conversations with an unknown stranger that led to Justin's conversion to Christianity. The bulk of the *Dialogue* is Justin's account of his discussion with Trypho, in which Justin seeks to persuade Trypho of the truth of Christianity. For present purposes the main attention will be paid to chapters 10–33 which contain Justin's views on the validity of the Old Testament law.

Justin's observations are in response to Trypho's charge that, while professing to believe in God, Christians do not observe his commandments. Thus they do not practise circumcision, nor observe the Sabbath or the festivals. They reject God's covenant and are in no way different from other people in the way they conduct their lives, whereas Jews, who accept the covenant, live as people called to be distinct among the nations. Justin's reply is as follows. First, circumcision was not commanded by God until the time of Abraham. Adam was not circumcised, nor was Noah, Lot, Enoch or Melchizedek. When circumcision was commanded by Abraham it was a prophetic sign, a means whereby the Jews would become a separated nation and suffer just punishment for their rejection of God as revealed in Christ. That circumcision had nothing to do with faith was indicated by the fact that women could not be circumcised; yet God intended women to be able to observe all things that were righteous and virtuous.

Second, Justin used an argument that would be employed many times by Christian apologists. This was to the effect that the Old Testament law was given by God to the Israelites on account of their wickedness. This was true of the sacrificial system, the Sabbaths and festivals, and the avoidance of certain types of food. The law promulgated on Horeb pertained to the Israelites alone. It was not intended for the nations. For them, a new law has been revealed, namely Christ, which puts an end to the old law and covenant. The proof text for this is Jeremiah 31:31–32, in which the prophet speaks of a new covenant, a law written on the hearts of humankind. Christians would observe the Old Testament if they were ignorant of why it was given, but they are not ignorant. They know that it was given on account of the hardness of heart and the transgressions of the Jewish people. They know that it cannot apply to them.

The strong anti-Jewish tone of the *Dialogue*, for all that the conversation contained in it is conducted without rancour and in a spirit of fairness, must be seen in the context of Jewish-Christian relationships at the time of its composition. For present purposes, what is important is the way that Christian attitudes to Judaism, as reflected in the *Dialogue*, affect the evaluation of the Old Testament law. This was negative, and amounted to saying that it was not binding upon Christians.

Irenaeus (c.135–c.200), Bishop of Lyon, was a defender of Christian orthodoxy against two sets of teachings, among others those of Marcion and of the Gnostics. This he did in his major work *Against Heresies*. Marcion (c.85–c.1160) took to an extreme what he found in the writings of Paul, and rejected the Old Testament and its law so completely that the church founded by him recognized as scripture only the Gospel of Luke and seven letters of Paul. Marcion believed that the Old Testament revealed an inferior god, who had created the world, but who was a merciless judge. Under his regime mankind, weakened by sin, was unable to fulfil the commands of this god and suffered accordingly. The God revealed by Jesus was a higher God whose mercy and love offered salvation. Marcion was partly influenced in his estimation of the Old Testament by philosophical beliefs in the necessary perfection of divinity, and of its freedom from human passions and vacillations. Old Testament language about God, given these philosophical assumptions, seemed to point to a deity that could not be God in the purest and highest sense. The Gnostics, whose teachings were far from uniform, made similar philosophical assumptions about the nature of deity, but did not see Paul, or part of his teaching, as providing the key to a true understanding of the gospel.

Marcion threw down a challenge not only to his contemporaries, but also indirectly to interpreters in all subsequent ages. What is one to make of the apparent moral crudities attributed to God in the Old Testament? How can such a text as the Old Testament offer moral advice to Christians living in more enlightened circumstances and more modern times? Marcion's strategy was to reject the Old Testament entirely, as a revelation stemming from a god other than the God of Jesus. Interpreters from the third century onwards, as we shall see, appealed to a spiritual, deeper, sense of the Old Testament as containing its authentic message. At and after the Reformation, when the "literal" sense of the Bible once more came into its own, various strategies were devised to defend the morality of God in the

Old Testament, procedures that endured until the nineteenth century, when the moral difficulties were explained in evolutionary terms, as evidence for ancient Israel's development from crude, "primitive" notions of God to the lofty ideals of the prophets. These developments will be described in later chapters. For the moment, the main concern will be with how Irenaeus answered Marcion; but this small diversion has sufficed to show that addressing critical questions to the biblical text and assessing it in the light of contemporary philosophy and ethics is not a procedure that was first invented in "liberal" circles in the nineteenth and twentieth centuries.

In order to meet Marcion's rejection of the Old Testament Irenaeus needed to affirm it, to show how it had been in some ways fulfilled and surpassed by the New Testament, and how at least the Decalogue or Ten Commandments were binding universally. The necessary link between the two testaments was established by the prophecies of Christ's coming, and how certain Old Testament events pointed symbolically to Christ (*Against Heresies* 4.9–11). The Old Testament laws had been disclosed to Israel as an expression of God's love, and as a way of enabling the Israelites to advance from less important, to more significant principles and precepts (*Against Heresies* 4.14.2–3). Prior to the time of Moses, righteous men from Adam to Abraham lived without circumcision, and with God's laws written on their hearts (4.16). Circumcision was given to Abraham as a sign that would enable his descendants to be a recognizable people. The same was true of observance of the Sabbath. Moses, originally, demanded only observance of the Ten Commandments (4.15.1, quoting Deut. 5:22 especially the words "and he added no more"). However, following the apostasies of the people, especially in making the Golden Calf (Exod. 32) other precepts were added, the proof being the statement in Matthew 19:8, that the law about divorce was given through Moses because of the "hardness of heart" of the Israelites. The Old Testament laws, then, apart from the Ten Commandments, were promulgated in special circumstances that no longer applied to Christians. However, the Ten Commandments continue to have validity: generally, because they command love of God and love of one's neighbour (4.16.3) and because of the way in which they have been widened in scope by the teaching of Jesus. Here Irenaeus refers to Matthew 5:22–28, where murder is redefined in terms of unjustified anger, and adultery is redefined in terms of lust. Indeed, one of Irenaeus' strongest arguments against Marcion was the fact that Jesus claimed to fulfil the Old Testament law and not to destroy it (Matt. 5:17–18). This meant that while Jesus rejected the traditions of the elders (Mark 7:3), he affirmed those parts of the law that accorded with the natural precepts of law (4.13). This is a view that would be important in subsequent Christian interpretation; and it indicated a slight movement towards a more positive attitude to the Old Testament law.

Chapter 5

FROM THE THIRD CENTURY TO THE REFORMATION

1. *Clement of Alexandria and Origen*

The task of the great exegetes associated with Alexandria, Clement (c.150–215) and Origen (c.185–254) – although Origen would later establish himself in Caesarea on the coast of Palestine – was to commend Christianity to Greek philosophers and to argue that the wisdom contained in the Bible was older than Greek philosophy, had influenced the latter, and was superior to it. This required a positive attitude to the Old Testament, and especially to Moses. The implications for the Old Testament law were that it was allegorized or spiritualized. In this regard the Christian interpreters had a forerunner in the great Jewish exegete of Alexandria, Philo (20/10 BCE–c.45 CE). In *The Instructor* (or *Paedagogos*), Clement argues that the author of the whole Bible is the divine Word who became incarnate in Jesus. It was this divine Word who communed with Abraham, wrestled with Jacob (Gen. 32:22–32) and spoke to Moses. It was he who said, "I am the Lord thy God, that brought thee out of the land of Egypt" (Exod. 20:1). However, the fact that the same divine Word was the author of the whole Bible does not mean that all its teaching is of equal validity. The older people (the Jews) had an Old Covenant in which the people were disciplined by the law, and the Word appeared as an angel. But there is now a New Covenant. The fear that characterized the Old Covenant has been turned to love, and the Word has appeared in Jesus. In contrasting the temporary Old Covenant with the permanent New Covenant, Clement makes much of the passage in John 1:17: "the law was given through Moses, grace and truth came through Jesus Christ." The contrast between law, on the one hand, and grace and truth, on the other, indicates the superiority of the New Covenant, as does the fact that the former covenant was given via an intermediary (Moses) while the New Covenant is given directly by the Word incarnate.

An interesting feature of *The Instructor* is that it gives advice on how to live as a Christian. The subjects dealt with include eating, drinking, dressing, personal appearance, conduct at feasts and banquets, public behaviour, church-going, and behaviour out of church. While there are various allusions to the Bible, including a significant proportion of references to Ecclesiasticus (Ben Sirah), there is only a passing reference to the Ten Commandments. On the whole, Clement urges moderation and modesty in all things, with particular emphasis on women preferring to cultivate the beauty of virtue and spirituality, rather than relying on external adornments such as makeup, jewellery and fine clothes. The Ten Commandments are presented as a simple and straightforward list of sins to be avoided, and include the injunction "thou shalt not corrupt boys." But the commandments are supplemented by other passages from the Old and New Testaments which demand compassion and social justice (e.g., Isa. 1:16–18; 58:7–9). The so-called household codes (e.g., Eph. 4:25–29; 6:4–9) are also invoked. The overall impression gained is that Clement's vision of ideal Christian behaviour owes much to the Greek philosophers, but that it is set within a Christian context which also draws upon the Bible (for Clement this is the Greek Bible including the so-called Apocrypha) where appropriate. Where biblical commandments can be applied literally, this is then done. Where they appear to be impractical (or immoral) they are allegorized or spiritualized.

In Book II chapter 18 of *The Miscellanies* Clement expands his argument about Moses being the precursor and finest exemplar of the highest virtues of Greek philosophy by arguing that the Mosaic law is the source from which the Greeks drew their knowledge of ethical values. However, his appeal to the laws of Moses is shaped by an agenda taken from the Greeks, with especial mention of Pythagoras. In other words, if the laws of Moses have validity it is because they are examples of teachings also disseminated widely among the Greeks. The key word in Clement's exposition is manliness, a virtue that includes patience, magnanimity and caution. The first of the Mosaic laws that commands manliness is that in Deuteronomy 22:5, which prohibits a man from wearing women's clothes. It means that a man is not to be effeminate in thought, or word or deed. This is followed by the law that permits a man to be excused from the field of battle in time of war, if he has a newly-built but not yet dedicated house, or a vineyard whose fruit he has not yet enjoyed, or is betrothed but not yet married (Deut. 20:5–7). The reason for his being excused military service is so that he may benefit from the house, vineyard and bride-to-be, a situation that will point to the manliness of his soul. The dangers of being effeminate are illustrated from the incident in Numbers 31:1–20, where the Israelites, in their war against Midian, capture but do not kill some of the Midianite women, and have intercourse with them. This provokes drastic action on the part of Moses, which involves killing the Midianite women who have had intercourse with Israelites. This saves the people from falling into the power of the enemy.

A second main heading under which the Mosaic law is considered is that of community and communication. The first law to be cited is that which forbids usury (Deut. 23:19). Magnanimity (one of the aspects of manliness) requires charity. This not only rules out usury, but entails the laws that require fields and vineyards not to be completely harvested, so that the poor may benefit from what is deliberately left (Lev. 19:9–10). Tithes of fruit and flocks are also ways of preventing greed. Again, the jubilee year (Lev. 25:10), in which estranged land is returned to its original owners, is a curb against coveting possessions. Other ways in which respect and love of one's neighbours are commanded are in the laws about returning the lost beast even of an enemy (Exod. 23:4; Deut. 22:1–3), not having intercourse with a female captive (Deut: 20:10–14), and showing compassion to animals. Much of the discussion of this last point is taken from pagan writers, particularly Pythagoras, but the biblical injunctions include not seething a kid in its mother's milk (Deut. 14:21), not muzzling an ox when it treads the grain (Deut. 25:4) and not yoking together an ox and an ass (Deut. 22:10).

While many readers today will not warm to Clement's views on manliness and the perils of being effeminate, it is hard not to be struck by his stress upon generosity and compassion. Further, it is striking that so many examples are taken from those parts of the Pentateuch that exude a spirit of grace rather than of law. These are commandments that commend themselves precisely because of their humanitarian appeal. Taken mostly at the level of the letter or their plain meaning, they can be cited without embarrassment; yet their spiritual sense is never far away, in Clement's hands. The law about not yoking together an ox and an ass is also taken to mean that it is wrong to bring a person of one race under the yoke of that which belongs to a different race. However, it is with Origen that we find some remarkable spiritualizing of Old Testament laws.

Origen is the master of this type of approach, and his method will be illustrated from his *Homilies on Exodus* in which there is a long discussion of Exodus 21:22–25. The passage reads as follows, in the Latin translation of Origen's works by Rufinus: "When two men quarrel and injure a pregnant woman and her child is born unformed [i.e., she has a miscarriage], the one causing the harm will be liable to compensation fixed by the husband and he will pay an honourable fine. If it is born deformed, he will give life for life, eye for eye, tooth for tooth, hand for hand, foot for foot, burning for burning, wound for wound, stripe for stripe" (*Homilies on Exodus* 10.1; my translation). Origen's first observation is that not all things that are commanded in the Bible are "law." Quoting Psalm 19:7–9 (Greek: Ps. 18:8–9) Origen notes the different terms that are employed there in addition to the word "law," namely, "testimony," "justice," "precepts," "fear" and "judgements." The purpose of this is to point out that the passage under consideration comes under the heading not of "law" but of "justices" (*Iustitiae*), the term found at the beginning of Exodus 21 (v. 1). While the significance of these different terms is not followed up, Origen's observation is a reminder even to modern readers of the Bible that a variety of terms is used to describe the things that God commands.

Origen's next point is that Jesus, in Matthew 5:38, gives the passage a new meaning by counselling non-violence, and turning the other cheek. This raises the question, does the quotation "an eye for an eye and a tooth for a tooth" in Matthew 5:38 come from Exodus 21:24 or from Deuteronomy 19:21 where the words occur in the quite different context (compared with Exodus 21:24) of the punishments appropriate to those who give false evidence in court? Origen is unable to decide; but he has established a difficulty about how the words are to be understood given the different contexts in which they occur. He now turns to the difficulties that are latent in Exodus 21:22–25.

First, if *two* men are involved in the fight in which the pregnant woman is injured, why is only *one* required to pay compensation? What is the "honourable compensation"? In the case of the fully-formed infant being dead on birth, Origen can understand the meaning of "life for life." A murder has been committed, for which the punishment is death. What, however, is meant by "eye for eye and tooth for tooth"? Is it to be assumed that the blow that has caused the miscarriage has also injured the eye of the child in the womb? If this explanation is accepted, then what does the phrase about the tooth mean? Does the passage assume that the child in the womb already had teeth? Because these assumptions seem absurd, Origen considers other possible scenarios. Perhaps the blow that caused the miscarriage injured the woman and not the child. This may explain the eye and the tooth, but what about the burning? Did the woman intervene in the men's quarrel in such a way as to be burned? The unsatisfactory answers to these questions lead Origen to look at the Deuteronomy passage, where there are also difficulties. In what circumstances would a false witness, who should incur the penalty that his victim would have suffered if convicted on the basis of the false evidence, lose an eye or a tooth? What offences required such penalties? Having shown the impossibility of interpreting the passages at their face value in their contexts, Origen concludes that their meaning must be spiritual, quoting Romans 7:14 "we know that the law is spiritual."

Before Origen's spiritual interpretation is described it must be observed that the critical acumen that he displays is of the highest order, and that he demonstrates to any intelligent reader the absurdities of the passages in Exodus 21 and Deuteronomy 19, when taken at face value in their contexts. Modern commentators can deal with the difficulties by saying that the law of talion ("an eye for an eye," etc.) which is well known from other laws in the ancient Near East, has been inserted into the passages at convenient points in the manner common in the ancient world when laws are being collected together. Without such assumptions, it has to be allowed that Origen's case for the absurdity of the passages is unanswerable.

In spiritualizing the passage, Origen refers to other passages in the Bible where parts of the body have spiritual or figurative meanings. Thus the saying about not removing a speck from your brother's eye when you have a beam in your own eye (Matt. 7:3–4) is not to be taken literally. It follows that in Exodus 21:22–25, the womb of the woman is the place where the soul of a believer resides. The quarrel of the men is the disputations of experts about doctrinal and other matters. Origen (*Homilies* 10.3) quotes 2 Timothy 2:23–24, which in his Latin text reads: "avoid, therefore, questions of the law, knowing that they engender disputes. A servant of God should not dispute." The injured child is thus the soul of a believer that is injured as a result of disputes. "Life for life" is a case in which a believer has been led to follow teaching that leads away from Christian faith. The person responsible will be judged accordingly at the day of judgement. Injury to the eye is damage to the intelligence, injury to the teeth a hindering of spiritual nourishment and injury to the hand is impeding the soul's ability to do good rather than evil. Appropriate judgements for those responsible are envisaged. The reference to burning is damage that will lead to a soul facing the fires of Gehenna. Origen sums up the exposition by referring to 1 Timothy 3:3, which says that anyone who aspires to be a teacher in the church must not be violent, a commandment given to prevent such a teacher from striking a pregnant woman, that is, a believer who has received the word of faith.

2. *The* Apostolical Constitutions

The *Apostolical Constitutions* is a composite work generally held to have been compiled around 380 CE in Antioch (Metzger, 1985: 58–62). It contains versions of two earlier works, the *Didascalia (Teaching) of the Apostles* [chapters 1–6] and the *Didache* (chapter 7; see above, p. 23), and Canons (i.e., resolutions) collected from those made at the Councils of Antioch (c.340) and Laodicaea (c.360; chapter 8). It is thus an important witness to beliefs and practices in the Eastern Church of the period. Its approach to the Old Testament law is one of both rejection and acceptance, with theory and practice diverging. It is also evidence for the more literal approach to the Bible that characterized the churches of Syria as opposed to the allegorizing tendencies of Alexandria.

We begin with the theory. In chapters 19–29 of Book 6 a distinction is made between the First Law and the Second Law (or additional precepts). The First Law is the Decalogue (Ten Commandments) and what follows in Exodus 21–23. It is based on the law of nature, and is characterized by not being compulsive when dealing with positive commandments. Thus it does not say (in Exod. 20:24–25), "make me an altar," but "if you make me an altar." In actual fact, verse 24 *does* say, "make me an altar," while verse 25 says, "if you make an altar," and the author/compiler appears to have conflated the two verses! The Second Law was that given following the apostasy of the Israelites in making the Golden Calf (Exodus 32). This incident provoked the anger of God "and he bound them with unbreakable bonds and imposed upon them burdens and a hard collar" (4.20.6 – possibly alluding to Deut. 28:48: "he [God] will put a yoke of iron on your neck"). This Second Law and its "Additional Precepts" has been taken away by the coming of Christ. The First Law has been confirmed and is to be followed in the freedom that Christ brings. The abolition of the Second Law is confirmed by reference to the standard Old Testament passages (Isa. 1:11, Amos 5:23, Jer. 7:21, etc.) that denounce the sacrificial cult of ancient Israel. The confirmation of the First Law is demonstrated from the New Testament in such passages as Matthew 5:21–22 where murder is extended to cover anger, and so forth. Indeed, we find here (6.23.3) some interesting interpretations of the Ten Commandments. Thus, for example, the meaning of the Sabbath law is that Christians should consider the law of creation and the providence of God, and give thanks for these things.

This is the theory; and if it were strictly adhered to it would presumably exclude all the legislation that is imposed upon the Israelites subsequent to Exodus 32. In practice, this is not the case. For example, the command to love one's neighbour as oneself, which is referred to at 6.23.1 comes, of course, from Leviticus 19:18. In Book 2.5.4 one of the most important attainments of a bishop is that he should be able to distinguish carefully between the (original) law and the secondary legislation, or additional precepts, so that believers do not become bound by unnecessary bonds. What this amounts to in practice can only be discovered by gleanings from the whole work, including the two final parts, namely, the version of the *Didache* and the Canons. The *Didache*, for example, is much altered and expanded, especially by biblical quotations.

The *Apostolical Constitutions* begins with an injunction to abstain from all cupidity or covetousness (Greek, *pleoneksia*) and all injustice. The commandment about not coveting is quoted (Exod. 20:17), an injunction amplified by Isaiah 5:8 ("woe to those who join house to house") and Deuteronomy 27:17 ("cursed be he who removes his neighbour's landmark"). Next, adultery is condemned, followed by a discussion of what is seemly in a woman's behaviour and appearance. Men are advised not to "mar their beards" (Lev. 21:5). Further instructions to women draw extensively on texts from the book of Proverbs. Book 2, dealing with bishops and other clergy, assumes that passages in the Old Testament referring to priests and prophets are applicable to Christian clergy. Thus, Ezekiel's words about the necessity and responsibility of being a watchman (Ezek. 33:1–7) are cited as are the words of Jeremiah (Jer. 26:2a–3). The support of the clergy and the relief of the poor is justified from Old Testament passages about offering tithes and first-fruits to the sanctuary (Num. 18:8–20) while the necessity for the bishop to be supreme in matters that concern the altar is justified from the stories of Samuel condemning Saul for offering a sacrifice (1 Sam. 13:13) and Uzziah being smitten with leprosy for burning incense in the temple (2 Chron. 26:16–18). Uzziah's punishment is also used in Book 3.10 as the ground for not allowing any layperson to perform any office that pertains to priests, a prohibition further reinforced by reference to the fate of Korah and his companions, whose rebellion against Moses resulted in their being victims of an earthquake and fire (Num. 16:1–35).

The theory about the original and secondary laws in Book 6 has already been referred to. Following its appearance in chapters 19–22 there are some interesting sections in chapters 26–29. They are targeted against "heretics" who abuse the "law and the prophets." Of these, some avoid certain foods and argue against marriage, maintaining that procreating children is evil. This view is rebutted by citing Genesis 1:28, "be fruitful and multiply"; but it is immediately made clear that "unnatural" sexual relationships (i.e., same-sex relationships, fornication and adultery) are forbidden. Here, Old

Testament laws are to the fore. Leviticus 18:22 and 20:13 are cited against homosexuality, and Leviticus 20:10 against adultery. Further, Leviticus 15:19 and Ezekiel 18:6 are invoked as laws forbidding a man to have intercourse with a woman during her menstrual periods.

In the version of the *Didache* found in Book 7, Old Testament texts are cited to forbid magic and witchcraft (Exod. 22:18), and divination (Num. 23:23). Blood is to be avoided when eating meat (Deut. 15:23). In the Canons collected in Book 8 the prohibited degrees of marriage in Leviticus 18 and 20 are implied in the prohibition against a cleric marrying two sisters, or his brother's or sister's daughter (Canon 19). Exodus 22:28 ("You shall not speak evil of a ruler of your people") is interpreted to mean that a member of the (lower) clergy must not abuse a bishop. Clergy who eat meat with its blood in it, or meat from animals that have been killed by other animals or have died a natural death (cp. Gen. 9:4; Lev. 17:13–15; Deut. 15:23) are to be deprived from office; lay offenders will be suspended.

Looking back over this incomplete summary of Old Testament laws found in the *Apostolical Constitutions*, one has to be impressed by the extent of reference to them. However, it must be emphasized that they are quoted because they are held to express the natural law; that if they are binding upon Christians who have been freed by Christ from the law, they are binding not just because they occur in the Bible, but because they are also consonant with the natural law. The overall view of Christian and ecclesiastical discipline is shaped by a combination of philosophical and Christian theological insights, among which citations from the Old Testament law have a part to play. Although there may be more than superficial resemblances between what is found in the *Apostolical Constitutions* and treatises written in the Reformed tradition after the Reformation, the underlying theories of the two approaches are quite different.

3. Augustine of Hippo

A discussion of the Old Testament law in relation to the Christian faith is at the centre of *On the Spirit and the Letter*, written by Augustine in 412 CE in connection with controversy concerning the teachings of Pelagius. These will not be discussed here, nor the part that *On the Spirit* played in Augustine's rebuttal of Pelagius (see Burger, 1951). This section will concentrate on how Augustine saw the Old Testament law in the Christian life. The main discussion begins at chapter 13 (21).

Augustine begins by distinguishing between the "law of works," which does not exclude human glory, and the "law of faith," which does exclude it. At first sight, the former belongs to Judaism and the latter to Christianity because Christianity does not practise circumcision and the other observances commanded in the Old Testament law. Such a conclusion is to be rejected, not only because Paul declares that the law is good (Rom. 7:12) but because the commandment "thou shalt not covet" (Exod. 20:17) is cited a number of times in the New Testament (e.g., Luke 12:15; Rom. 7:7, 13:9) and must therefore belong to the law of faith. The difference between the two laws is summed up as follows. The law of works commands with threats what the law of faith secures by believing. The former says, "thou shalt not covet," the second says (here Augustine quotes the Latin version of Wisdom 8:21), "as I knew I could not otherwise be continent except God gave it, and this was also a point of wisdom, to know whose gift it was, I addressed myself to the Lord and besought him." In connection with the law of works God says, "do what I command"; in regard to the law of faith one says to God, "give what you command." It is clear from this that if any parts of the law of works apply in any way to Christians, this is under entirely different conditions compared with those that obtained under the law of works.

The next part of Augustine's argument is to determine what is meant in 2 Corinthians 3:6 when it says, "the letter kills but the Spirit gives life." What is meant by "the letter"? A possibility is that it means those parts of the law that Christians no longer observe, namely, circumcision and the observances connected with it. An argument in favour of this would be that the Ten Commandments, with the exception of the commandment about the Sabbath, are surely binding upon Christians. Not to serve idols or other gods, to honour one's parents, to abstain from adultery, murder, vows, false evidence and covetousness are surely things that Christians are to observe. The "letter that kills," the law of works, would therefore be the Old Testament law minus nine of the Ten Commandments. However, this conclusion is ruled out by what precedes 2 Corinthians 3:6, namely, "you are truly a letter of Christ, written by our ministry, not with ink but by the Spirit of the living God, not on tablets of stone but on tablets of human hearts" (2 Cor. 3:3). The reference to "tablets of stone," that is, the Ten Commandments, makes it certain that these are also "the letter that kills" three verses later. There is the slight possibility that the Corinthians passage is referring not to the Ten Commandments as a whole, but merely to the Sabbath commandment, but Augustine regards this as an absurd point of view.

It is by referring to Romans 7 that Augustine is able to square the circle; to argue that the nine of the Ten Commandments that must apply to Christians are also "the letter that kills," without being so for Christians. The function of the law in Romans 7 is to make sinful actions manifest and known. "If it had not been for the law, I should not have known sin" (Rom. 7:7). But the effect of this knowledge of sin is to make slaves of those who thus become aware of sin. The law does not convey the power to observe it. This is where the gospel and faith come in. They change completely the relationship between the believer and the law. What is done by the believer is done out of love, not fear. Thus, it is a gift of the Spirit of God, that enables a different principle to be at work within a believer, and which has a transforming effect on the believer's life day by day. The Ten Commandments, which were once written on tablets of stone by the finger of God, are now written on human hearts by the Spirit of God.

This transformed situation has two aspects. On the one hand, while the letter (e.g., nine of the Ten Commandments) still has force for Christians, the Spirit of God prevents this letter from killing. "Where the Spirit of the Lord is, there is freedom" (2 Cor. 3:17). Secondly, since the Spirit and faith are gifts from God, any thought that one can be proud of observing the Commandments, is excluded. This, incidentally, is what worried Augustine about the teaching of Pelagius. If it was admitted that a person, in principle, could live a blameless life without the help of God, this brought with it the danger that there would be pride in such an achievement. Such an attitude, according to Augustine, was a property of the law of works, not of the law of faith. In Romans 8:9, the observance of those of the Ten Commandments that refer to human relationships is summed up in the verse, "You shall love your neighbour as yourself." The love spoken of is not a human achievement but a response to the love of God.

The importance of *On the Spirit and the Letter* for the present work is the way in which it sets the whole status of the Old Testament law for Christians in the context of the doctrine of the Spirit of God. One can see already a distinction that would later be made explicit, between ceremonial commandments (e.g., circumcision, Sabbath, etc.) that are not binding on Christians and moral commandments (e.g., evidence of murder, etc.) that are. Yet it cannot be too strongly emphasized that the observance of the so-called moral commandments is entirely under the regime of the Spirit of God. If this is lacking, there is the ever-present danger of human pride, in which case the moral commandments will become a "letter that kills." This will need to be borne in mind in regard to later periods of interpreting the moral laws of the Old Testament.

This account of Augustine's treatise has necessarily omitted some of the other points made: that the Old Testament ceremonial observances point figuratively to the work of Christ, or that the Sabbath law in the Ten Commandments is a symbol of sanctification. There is a discussion of Jeremiah 31:31–34, in which a New Covenant is promised, when the law will be put within God's people and written on their hearts. While this is obvious support for Augustine's argument, he finds it necessary to comment on the words "they shall all know me, from the least of them to the greatest." Augustine takes the words to refer to the descendants of Israel, that is, the Church.

Another passage discussed by Augustine is Romans 2:14: "when the Gentiles who have not the law do by nature what the law requires, they are a law to themselves, even though they do not have the law." Whatever Paul may have intended to mean by this, the verse is potentially damaging to Augustine's standpoint. He had argued that a function of the law was to make sin known, yet here is a passage that speaks of people who do not possess the law, but yet who observe it. Further, the continuation of the passage (v. 15) says that what the law requires is written on their hearts – but this is precisely what Augustine claims for Christians through the agency of the Spirit of God. Is it therefore possible that there exist people who, apart from God's revelation to the Jews and the gift of God's Spirit through the gospel, know and observe a law written on their hearts? Augustine can only answer no, and defend his position by arguing that Romans 2:14–16 is speaking about Gentles converted to Christianity. Thus, he is able to maintain his view that salvation comes only through Christ. Whether or not one agrees with this from a modern perspective, what must not be overlooked is Augustine's stress on the role and dimension of the Spirit of God *within* the Christian view of salvation.

4. *Cyril of Alexandria*

Cyril was Archbishop of Alexandria from 412–444 CE. He is of interest to the present discussion because he introduced what might be called a dispensationalist view of Old Testament history. It is based upon Leviticus 19:23–25, which reads: "When you come into the land and plant all kinds of trees for fruit, then you shall count their fruit as forbidden to you, it must not be eaten... And in the fourth year all their fruit shall be holy, an offering of praise to the LORD. But in the fifth year you may eat of their fruit, that they may yield more richly for you." The usual explanation of this injunction is that the Israelites had noticed that fruit trees do not produce any or much fruit during their first three years and that they therefore stripped off the blossoms during these years in order to make the trees more productive. The fourth year was the first really productive year and the fruit produced in this year was dedicated to God as a kind of first-fruits offering. Whether or not this is correct, it is interesting that the Hebrew translated as "forbidden" is literally "uncircumcised" which invites the speculation that the three-year period of "uncircumcision" of the trees was seen as a transitional period during which the trees became part of the land owned by God (cp. Josh. 5:2–7 where the Israelites are circumcised a second time prior to their entrance into the promised land). It is not surprising that a law that still to some extent puzzles modern commentators should be given a spiritual interpretation by an early Christian exegete. Cyril took the five years of the cycle of the fruit trees to represent different periods in the history of Israel (see Kerrigan, 1952: 170–72). The first three years were the time of Moses, Joshua and the Judges, when the law was "impure, loaded with the coarseness of history and having the dark shadow around it as worthless refuse." The fourth year, the time of the prophets, was when some of the prophets set aside the law and looked forward to the advent of Christ. The passage in Hosea 6:6 – "I desire steadfast love and not sacrifice, the knowledge of God, rather than burnt offerings" meant that charity and the knowledge of Christ are more pleasing to God than animal sacrifices. Joel 1:13–19, containing the words "cereal offering and drink offering are withheld from the house of God" was taken to mean that the sacrifices instituted by Moses had ceased. During this fourth period the prophets were purifying the law and preparing it to be "eatable" during the fifth period, the coming of Christ.

5. Jewish and Christian Contacts

The next stage in Christian understanding of the Old Testament law that will be considered is that in which there was renewed interest among Christians in the literal sense of its commandments. This renewed interest was the result of contact between Christians and Jews. Indirectly, it paved the way for the interest in the Old Testament law that characterized the Reformation and post-Reformation periods. The next section will consider two Jewish exegetes, Abraham Ibn Ezra and Maimonides. The latter's work was translated into Latin and was this a powerful influence upon Christian theologians.

5a. *Abraham Ibn Ezra (1089–1164)*

Abraham Ibn Ezra was born in Spain, and became one of the greatest mediaeval Jewish commentators on the Bible, quite apart from also being a great poet. His biblical commentaries date from the 1140s, a period during which he travelled to Italy, France and Britain. He was an exponent of the literal interpretation of the Bible.

His commentary on the Ten Commandments (Ibn Ezra, 1976: 124–40) begins with a discussion of why they exist in two forms in Exodus 20:1–17 and Deuteronomy 5:6–21, versions that are not identical. Particular problems had long been caused to Jewish exegesis of the Ten Commandments by the fact that Exodus 20:8 required Jews to "remember" the Sabbath day while Deuteronomy 5:12 stated that Jews should "observe" the Sabbath (see Melammed, 1990). Other differences between the two versions were: the reason for observing the Sabbath day (because God rested on the Sabbath after creating the world, according to Exod. 20:11; in order to allow one's servants to rest, according to Deut. 5:14); the addition of the words "as the LORD your God commanded you" to the command to honour one's parents in Deuteronomy 5:16; the addition of "your ox and your ass" to the beneficiaries of the Sabbath-day rest at Deuteronomy 5:14, and the complete reshaping of the commandment about coveting in Deuteronomy 5:21. Whereas Exodus 20:17 speaks of not coveting your neighbour's house and not coveting your neighbour's wife and various other named possessions, Deuteronomy 5:21 begins with the command not to covet your neighbour's wife and then uses a different Hebrew verb as it goes on to say that a man should not *desire* his neighbour's house and other named possessions. How were these differences to be explained?

A traditional Jewish view was that God had spoken both versions in one utterance (see Melammed, 1990) but this did not satisfy Ibn Ezra's philosophical convictions. If this were so, how were the listeners supposed to understand "remember" and "observe" the Sabbath, since these verbs had different meanings? Ibn Ezra's answer, one that probably deliberately distanced him from Christian interpreters over the matter of how the Ten Commandments were to be numbered, was that God had *spoken* the version found in Exodus 20:1–17 and that the version found in Deuteronomy 5:6–21 was the words of Moses, words that included interpretative additions. This was justified on two grounds. First, Exodus 20:1 begins "God spoke these words…" whereas Deuteronomy 5:5 begins "he said," that is, in Deuteronomy it is *Moses* who is conveying to the Israelites what *God* had said. Second, the addition "as the LORD your God commanded you" in

Deuteronomy 5:16 made more sense as the words of Moses than as the words of God.

The view that God had spoken the Ten Commandments as found in Exodus 20 had an important bearing on how the commandments were numbered. The chief problem was whether what Protestant Christians take to be the first and second Commandments (having no other gods than the LORD and not making any graven image) were one commandment or two. Jewish and Catholic interpretation took them to be one, on the ground that the word "them" in "you shall not bow down to them" at Exodus 20:5 could only refer to the "other gods" at 20:3. If, however, Exodus 20:3–6 were *one* commandment, not two, how were there *ten* commandments? The traditional Christian answer to this problem was to regard Deuteronomy 5:21a – "you shall not covet your neighbour's wife" as the ninth commandment and Deuteronomy 5:21b – "you shall not desire your neighbour's house," and so on, as the tenth. Ibn Ezra's view, that only Exodus 20:1–17 represented what God said, ruled out this possibility. He affirmed, with traditional Jewish teaching, that the first commandment was Exodus 20:2 – "I am the LORD your God, who brought you out of the land of Egypt." Modern readers may be forgiven for thinking that it does not look like a commandment; but the phrase "Ten Commandments" is not biblical. The Bible's own name is Ten Words (Deut. 10:4 – cp. the name Decalogue), the Hebrew of which has been (mis-)translated as Ten Commandments in traditional English versions of the Bible.

Turning to note a few of the many observations that Ibn Ezra makes on the Decalogue, he interprets the "double" commandment regarding the Sabbath as follows. "Remember" (Exod. 20:8) is something that should be done for six days of the week. It should always be remembered that the Sabbath day is to be kept holy. "Observe" (Deut. 5:12) is what is to be done on the day itself. The command to do no murder (Exod. 20:13) is held to cover not only what might be done with one's hands, but what can be done with the tongue. False witness and gossip are included in the prohibition. In commenting on "You shall not commit adultery" (Exod. 20:14), Ibn Ezra refers to his great predecessor Saadia Gaon (882–942), erstwhile head of the rabbinic academy in Sura, Babylon. Saadia distinguished several types of sexual abuse under this heading, rising in successive degrees of severity. The lowest was intercourse with a virgin or widow, followed by intercourse with one's menstruating wife, then a married woman, then a Canaanite (foreign) woman, then with another male, then with an animal. The reason for the degrees of severity was that while intercourse with one's menstruating wife, another man's wife or a foreign woman involved prohibitions that might become possibilities (the menstrual period would end, the married woman might be widowed and become available for marriage, the foreign woman might enter the Jewish community – each possibility being more remote than the preceding one), there was no way in which a man or an animal could become a legitimate object of sexual intercourse. Ibn Ezra observed that, in actual fact, the same penalty was prescribed for each of these offences; but the fact that he quoted the opinion of Saadia indicates his willingness to think profoundly about the implications of the commandments, and what they might refer to.

The commandment not to steal (Exod. 20:15) was similarly seen to cover a number of different activities. Basically, it meant secretly taking another's possessions; but it could also cover stealing a man (Exod. 21:16), that is, depriving people of their liberty, cheating people by using false weights or measurements (cp. Amos 8:5) or stealing people's hearts (i.e., falsely gaining people's allegiance, as Absalom did when planning his revolt against David in 2 Sam. 15:1–6). The commandment about not coveting is also interestingly dealt with. Ibn Ezra recognizes its inherent difficulty. How can one *not* desire something that is beautiful to look at? He answers by referring to things that people do not desire or covet, because they are unobtainable. A peasant does not covet sleeping with a beautiful princess, or having wings to fly, like a bird. A man has no desire to sleep with his mother, even if she is beautiful. He knows that such a thing is not done. Not to covet therefore means not to desire those things that are unobtainable. Further, it means to be content with the lot that one has been given by God.

5b. *Moses Maimonides (1135–1204)*

Moses Maimonides, who was born in Cordoba, Spain and spent much of his later life in Cairo working as a physician, completed his great work *Dalalat al-Hairin* (*The Guide of the Perplexed*) in Arabic in 1190. It has been recognized as one of the most important works ever written on Jewish faith and philosophy. It was profoundly influenced by the writings of Aristotle as interpreted by the Arabic philosophers of the time.

The law as found in the Old Testament is discussed in Part III from chapter 26 of the Guide. Maimonides distinguishes between statutes (Hebrew, *huqqim*) and judgements (Hebrew, *mishpatim*). In the former, it is not immediately clear what the purpose is. Examples include the law in Leviticus 19:23–25 about fruit trees (see above, p. 00) and about not sewing vineyards with two kinds of seed (Deut. 22:9). The purpose of the judgements, for example the prohibitions of killing or stealing, is obvious

(Pines, 1963: 507; Kapach, 1972: 553). However, it should not be supposed that the statutes do not have a purpose, or that attempts to discover their purpose should not be made, even though in some cases no answer will be found. For example, it is clear that animals may be killed for food because this will benefit the human race. The fact that they are to be killed in a certain way is a merciful provision to enable the killing to be as easy and painless as possible. On the other hand, it is unlikely that reason will be able to discover why a lamb is required for one particular sacrifice and a ram for another.

Having made the distinction between statutes and judgements, Maimonides discusses commandments (Hebrew, *mitsvoth*), again arguing that the purpose of some is obvious while the cause of others is obscure. Some commandments have three purposes: to abolish reciprocal wrongdoing, to urge a "noble moral quality" that leads to good social and civic relationships, and to communicate a correct opinion or belief. The latter will include correct belief about the unity and purposes of God. Such commandments display clear reasons and aims: "No one was ever so perplexed for a day as to ask why we were commanded by the law that God is one, or why we were forbidden to kill and to steal, or why we were forbidden to exercise vengeance and retaliation, or why we were ordered to love one another" (Pines, 1963: 513: Kapach, 1972: 559–560). But what about other commandments, such as the prohibition of wearing garments made of two types of material, such as wool and linen (Deut. 22:11)? Here, Maimonides reminds his readers that Abraham grew up among "Sabians," that is, pagans, and that he exiled himself from them in response to a prophetic revelation (Gen. 12:1–3). Maimonides refers to a work entitled "The Nabatean Agriculture" believed by him to have been translated by a certain Ibn Wahshiyya. Apparently this work was compiled from various sources by Ibn Wahshiyya around 904 (Pines, 1963: 518 note 25; Kapach, 1972: 565 note 59), and was a prime source for knowledge of the beliefs of the "Sabians." Other works such as " ᵓal-Ustumakhus" (allegedly written by Aristotle, but not accepted as authentic by Maimonides) and a work by a certain Ishaq al-Sabi are mentioned as sources for knowledge of the laws and religion of the Sabians. Maimonides uses the information gained from these sources to argue that many seemingly pointless commandments in the Jewish law were actually direct contradictions of pagan practices and beliefs. Their purpose was to prevent the Jews from adopting pagan practices, and from falling into idolatry. Thus the law in Leviticus 19:23–25 about the fruit of trees newly planted in the Holy Land was framed in direct opposition to pagan practices. The latter demanded that the first fruits on any edible tree should be sacrificed to false gods, the remaining fruit being eaten in idolatrous temples. The Jewish law ordered that the fruits of the first three years should be destroyed.

Another approach to explaining the laws, used by Maimonides, is the analogy of growing up, whereby a child progresses in its foods from liquids until it can eat solids (compare the similar argument in I Pet. 2:2). "Many things in our Law are due to something similar to this very Government," wrote Maimonides (Pines, 1963: 525; Kapach, 1972: 574), arguing that human beings cannot suddenly change from one way of life to another. A text used to justify this view was Exodus 13:17–18: "God led them not by the way of the land of the Philistines, although it was near…but God led the people about by the way of the wilderness of the Red Sea." The reference is to the devious route by which the Israelites progressed to the Promised Land, the point being that it would have been impossible for people, who immediately prior to their departure from Egypt had been slaves working with clay and bricks, to undertake the task of forcefully occupying the Promised Land without any training or preparation. Similarly, some of the laws given through Moses were by way of training and preparation with the aim that the people might arrive at a greater reverence for God. An implication of this is that some of the sacrificial cult partook of what might be called a transitional purpose, and Maimonides was able to invoke texts that had been used by Christian writers to discredit the whole sacrificial system. A key text here was Jeremiah 7:22–23: "I spoke not unto your Fathers, nor commanded them, in the day that I brought them out of the land of Egypt, concerning burnt offerings or sacrifices; but this thing commanded I them, saying: Harken unto my voice and I will be your God, and you shall be my people." Maimonides explained this by saying that the sacrificial laws were given only in order to enable the fundamental principles to be realized: that the people should know and worship God. The sacrificial laws were therefore a means to an end, and not an end in themselves. To the objection, why could God not confer upon his people the ability to know and observe the fundamental principles towards which the law aimed, Maimonides answered that it was not the will of God that human nature should be altered in a miraculous way. "If it were His will that the nature of any human individual should be changed because of what He…wills, the sending of prophets and all giving of a law would have been useless." (Pines, 1963: 529; Kapach, 1972: 578). This sketch of Maimonides' account of the law has omitted consideration of the long section, chapters 35–49 of Part III, in which the commandments are divided into 14 classes, each of which is then discussed fully. The aim here has been to give an idea of the overall approach in *The Guide*, which was to deal honestly with apparent difficulties and obscurities in the laws in a reasoned way, without compromising the belief that the laws represented the highest will of the only true God. The work of Maimonides ensured that while Christians still regarded the Old Testament law as fulfilled or superseded in Christ, they could no longer use its apparent illogicalities at some points to argue that its *true* meaning was allegorical or spiritual. Of course, spiritual meanings could be discerned in the Old Testament law, but this was rooted as far back as the New Testament, and writings such as the letter to the Hebrews. But the literal meaning also made sense within the Jewish context for which it had been intended. *The Guide of the Perplexed* was studied carefully by subsequent Christian writers and by none more so than the scholar whose work is considered in the next section.

6. *Aquinas*

Thomas Aquinas (1224/25–1274) is regarded as one of the greatest and most important theologians in the history of Christianity. He was also one of the most profound thinkers on the nature of morality in general and the place of the Bible in morality in particular. He was born not far from Naples to the Count of Aquino, entered the Dominican Order in Naples in 1244 and spent much of his life teaching in the University of Paris. His *Summa Theologica*, which will be discussed here, was composed in Paris and Italy between 1265 and 1273. The "Treatise on the Law" in Part II occupies questions 90–108. Although essentially a theological work, the *Summa* is broadly conceived. The sections on law make reference to "The Philosopher," that is, Aristotle and the latter's *Nicomachean Ethics* and *Politics*. In the discussion of the ceremonial commandments of the old law (i.e., that in the Old Testament) there are frequent references to "Rabbi Moses," that is, Maimonides and to *The Guide of the Perplexed*. The importance of Aquinas' treatment of the moral teaching of the Bible is the way in which he sets this within a general theory of morality, which provides him with criteria for evaluating and interpreting the biblical material.

For those unfamiliar with the *Summa* and its methods, it proceeds by answering questions, which are formulated by a series of objections to the point or points that Aquinas wishes to maintain. These objections articulate and draw attention to every difficulty, problem, contradiction or obscurity that could be imagined concerning the matter under discussion, and indicate a profound level of critical engagement with the subject. Following the statement of the objections, Aquinas puts forward a general viewpoint that contradicts the tenor of the objections, before dealing with each one in detail. The argument is conducted in a logical and humane manner throughout. In what follows it will not be possible to reproduce Aquinas' procedure, nor to do any more than touch briefly on matters that are treated in great detail (see for the text, Aquinas, 1927).

Fundamental to the whole discussion is the distinction between natural law, human law and divine law. Natural law is that which is known to all human beings by the exercise of reason. Of course, its source is God, who, as the creator of the universe and of human kind, has brought into being a rational world populated by rational beings. In this rational world all things and institutions are designed to serve and achieve specific ends. That of human kind is happiness, which also has a social and eternal dimension. Natural law discloses general principles, such as that it is wrong for one human being to harm another. It is the task of human law to give more specific and concrete expression to these general principles. The precept "not to murder" would be a concrete expression in human law of the general principle in natural law, that no human should harm another. An important consequence of the distinction between natural and human law is that while the former can never change, the latter can. Obviously, if natural law is, so to speak, built into the very constitution of the universe and its inhabitants, natural law could only change if the universe changed. Human law, on the other hand, is precisely the work of humans, in specific circumstances and times. As these change and develop, so the specific ways in which the principles of natural law are worked out may change and develop. An example would be modes of government, which are required to regulate the social lives of human beings. Some peoples are ruled by kings, others by elected or unelected groups of powerful people and others by arrangements that allow free citizens to express and fulfil their wishes. Exactly how people are governed is the province of human law; and if a people changes one form of government for another, it will also change the laws that are appropriate to the new form of government as opposed to the old.

Divine law is either revealed by God or discerned prophetically by inspired or wise teachers. It has several functions. One is to make known the principles of the natural law in cases where failures in human behaviour or understanding have damaged the possibility of it being discerned. Another is to communicate religious information, about the nature of God and about rites and ceremonies that will enable people to worship and serve him. Divine law can also override commandments derived from natural law. Three examples of this cited by Aquinas come from the Old

Testament: God's command to Abraham to sacrifice his son Isaac (Gen. 22:2), God's command to the Jews in Egypt to borrow and purloin vessels from the Egyptians at the time of the Exodus (Exod. 12:35) and the command to the prophet Hosea to take "a wife of fornications" (Hos. 1:2; i.e., to marry a prostitute) (Question 94 article 5: Aquinas 49). Aquinas' answer is, in effect, that what God commands must be right by definition. Since God is the lord of life and property, he can decide on the life or death of anyone without injustice: and if God commands someone to have intercourse with a woman or to take someone else's property, the actions are not fornication, adultery or theft.

The identification of the natural, human and divine laws makes possible the division of the commandments in the Old Testament into moral, ceremonial and judicial commandments. To be sure, Aquinas was not the first Christian theologian, and by no means the last, to make this division; but the way in which he grounded the division in his overall theory was important. Moral commandments, found especially in the Ten Commandments in injunctions such as "you shall do no murder" were derived from the natural law via human law, and as such were binding upon all mankind. It is important to note that they were not binding because they were to be found in the Bible: they were binding because they derived from the natural law. The ceremonial prescriptions came from divine law, and were given specifically to the Israelites in order to direct their lives and worship away from idolatry and pagan practices and towards God. In describing and defending their rationale, Aquinas drew extensively upon *The Guide of the Perplexed.* We find repeated from *The Guide* the justification, for example, of the law about fruit trees in Leviticus 19:23–25 (see above, p. 43). However, Aquinas added a dimension that could not have occurred in *The Guide,* namely, the view that the ceremonies pointed to the coming, nature and sacrifice of Christ. Again, this was not new in Christian interpretation of the Old Testament, but the whole approach was new insofar as the ceremonies were attributed to divine law, which meant that they could not be regarded as arbitrary or irrational in their original setting in ancient Israel. A typical example of Aquinas' typological approach occurs in his discussion of why certain animals and materials were specified for particular sacrifices and ceremonies. Having justified these on rational grounds, Aquinas writes: "Thirdly, it was fitting that these animals should be offered that they might foreshadow Christ. Because, as the same gloss observes [here Aquinas quotes from the *Glossa Ordinaria* on Lev. 1] *Christ is offered in the calf, to denote the strength of the cross: in the lamb, to signify His innocence: in the ram, to foreshadow His headship:*

in the goat to signify the likeness of simple flesh. The turtle dove and dove denoted the union of the two natures: or else the turtle dove signified chastity: while the dove was a figure of charity. *The wheat-flour foreshadowed the sprinkling of believers with the water of Baptism"* (Question 102 article 2: Aquinas 168–69). An implication of Aquinas' understanding of the ceremonial law that was with the coming of the New Law, that of Christ, any observance by Christians of the old ceremonial law was tantamount to apostasy. It was to reject the Gospel, which had been revealed by the divine law, in favour of that which merely pointed to the Gospel.

The view that Christian observance of the old law would in fact be a mortal sin (Question 103 article 4: Aquinas 234) raised several difficulties about the behaviour of the first followers of Jesus. Peter had refused to eat with Gentiles at Antioch (Gal. 2:12) and the Council of Jerusalem had obliged Gentile converts to observe the Old Testaments laws about not eating blood and abstaining from fornication (Acts 15:20, 29). Aquinas rejected the view of Jerome that the apostles had pretended to observe the Jewish ceremonies so as not to hinder the conversion of Jews to Christianity. Aquinas preferred the view of Augustine who had argued that during the period of Christ's earthly ministry until the crucifixion, the ceremonies of the old law could be observed. After the proclamation of the Gospel by the Apostles, observance of the Jewish ceremonies was a deadly sin, except for Jewish converts, provided that they did not put their trust in them. This explained some of the behaviour of the apostles, for example, that Paul circumcised Timothy (Acts 16:3). In fact, the reason why the Holy Spirit allowed converted Jews to observe the ceremonies, while converted Gentiles were forbidden to do so, was to indicate that the Jewish ceremonies pointed typologically to Christ, whereas heathen ceremonies did not. On the matter of the prohibition of blood to gentile converts, Aquinas held that its aim was not to uphold a legal ceremony from the old law, but to help Jewish and Gentile Christians to live amicably with each other. As time went on, the eating of meat without the blood having first being drained ceased to be a divisive issue, and the saying of Jesus was accepted that no one can be defiled morally by what they eat (Matt. 15:11). The prohibition of fornication by the council of Jerusalem was a special case, because Gentiles did not believe that fornication was sinful.

How did the coming of Christ affect the judicial commandments of the old law? As with the ceremonial commandments, Aquinas began by defending their value within their setting in ancient Israel. In his opinion, the best form of government was that in which rulers were chosen by those who were ruled (Question 105 article 1: Aquinas 250). Aquinas argued that this kind of polity could be found in the Old Testament in passages such as Deuteronomy 1:13, where Moses called upon the people to choose men who would assist him in leading the nation. However, the judicial commandments were not only excellent in their situation: they also had a figurative significance. They governed people chosen specially by God, the people from among whom Christ would be born. Thus the mode of government and the deeds of the chosen people had a prophetic and figurative significance in a way that the deeds and wars of the Assyrians and Romans did not.

The coming of the new law affected the judicial commandments differently from the way in which the ceremonial precepts were affected. They were, of course, annulled by Christ's coming, but to observe them as Christian was not necessarily a deadly sin. "If a sovereign," wrote Aquinas, "were to order these judicial precepts to be observed in his kingdom, he would not sin: unless per chance they were observed, or ordered to be observed, as though they derived their binding force by being institutions of the old law: for it would be a deadly sin to intend to observe them thus" (Question 104 article 3: Aquinas 244). After the Reformation attempts were made to do precisely what Aquinas here condemned.

The section on Aquinas will conclude by noting some of his comments on the Ten Commandments.

Article 3 of Question 100 (Aquinas 117–19) discusses whether all the moral precepts of the old law can be found in reduced form in the Ten Commandments. Two objections that are considered are, firstly, that Jesus' summary of the principal precepts of the Law in Matthew 22:37, 39 – You shall love the Lord your God... You shall love your neighbour as yourself – are not found in the Ten Commandments; second, that the Sabbath commandment is a ceremonial, not a moral commandment. Aquinas' reply is that although the Ten Commandments are a special case, having been given by God to Moses, they are consistent with the primary principles of natural law. For example, the command not to kill is a specific application of the natural law principle that one should do no evil to another person. The fact that the two primary principles of love to God and to neighbour, are not explicitly stated in the Ten Commandments does not mean that they are not implied in them. With regard to the Sabbath commandment, it has a moral aspect in requiring a part of human time to be devoted to the things of God. An interesting observation of Aquinas is that the Gloss on Matthew 5:11 says that after he had propounded the ten precepts (i.e., Commandments) Moses set them out in detail. For Aquinas this was proof

that the moral precepts of the old law were reducible to the Ten
Commandments; but the observation is confirmed by modern critical work
on Deuteronomy, which sees chapters 6 and onwards as an exposition of
the Decalogue, which occurs in chapter 5 (e.g., Braulik, 1986).

Article 4 of Question 100 (Aquinas 119–222) deals, among other things,
with the numbering of the commandments, recognizing the problems
involved, and in particular whether Exodus 20:3–4 – You shall have no
other gods... You shall not make for yourself a graven image – constitutes
one commandment or two. Aquinas follows Augustine (*De quaestionibus
Exodii* 70; CC Series Latina 33.102–104) who argues not unreasonably
that the making of a graven image, and so on, is forbidden in relation to it
being worshipped as a god, and that Exodus 20:3–5 is therefore one
commandment. This entails, of course turning to Deuteronomy 5:21 to
provide commandments nine and ten. Aquinas follows Augustine in
distinguishing between the prohibition of carnal knowledge (not coveting
the wife of one's neighbour) and concupiscence of the eyes (not coveting
the house of one's neighbour, etc.).

Article 8 of Question 100 (Aquinas 133–36) discusses whether some of
the Ten Commandments are dispensable (i.e., not always universally
binding). Two examples given in the objections concern the command to
do no murder, which is apparently broken when evil-doers are executed, or
enemies are killed in warfare, and the Sabbath command. The objection
refers to the incident in 1 Maccabees 2:4, when the Jews decide to fight on
the Sabbath day rather than let themselves be slaughtered by their enemies.
Aquinas accepts that it is sometimes necessary to dispense (i.e., not observe)
a law if observing it would frustrate the primary principle that it is meant
to uphold. He argues, however, that the case is different with the Ten
Commandments. The execution of evil-doers and the killing of enemies
in war are ways of upholding the common good, and do not transgress the
command to do no murder. Similarly, if a person's property is lawfully
taken from him for the common good, this is not theft. Aquinas then refers
to the three cases cited earlier: God's command to Abraham to sacrifice
Isaac (Gen. 22), the command to the Israelites to purloin vessels from the
Egyptians (Exod. 12:35–36) and the command to Hosea to marry an
adulterous woman (Hos. 1:2). All these instances taken together show that
while the essential principles enshrined in the Ten Commandments cannot
be changed, particular applications of them may be dispensed by divine
law (as in the case of Abraham) and by human law (as in the lawful execution
of a criminal). On the matter of the Jews breaking the Sabbath law during
the Maccabean revolt, Aquinas argues that the law was not being broken

but interpreted. To do something for human welfare on the Sabbath is not to violate it. Aquinas refers to the teaching of Jesus in Matthew 12:3–8.

Aquinas' discussion of the law in the *Summa theologica* represents a high point in the theology of the pre-Reformation period. Grounded in a general theory of law with universal application and implications, it respects the dimension of divine revelation in the Bible, while at the same time situating this revelation within the general theory. The Old Testament laws are seen as valuable in their setting in ancient Israel, and as pointing forwards to the coming of the new law in Christ. How they are affected by this new revelation is carefully spelled out by way of the distinction between the moral, ceremonial and judicial precepts. At the same, the details of the Old Testament law are not overlooked. Their difficulties and apparent contradictions and inconsistencies are faced fairly and squarely, and the solutions put forward are convincing given the constraints and limitations of knowledge at the time in which Aquinas worked. The standards that he set were rarely equalled in subsequent scholarship and probably never surpassed. He is an object-lesson even and especially for modern users of the Bible in social and moral questions warning against a superficial use of the biblical text, both in interpretation and application.

Chapter 6

THE REFORMATION

1. *Luther*

To jump from Aquinas to Luther is to pass silently over some two hundred and fifty years. If the present work was attempting a comprehensive history of the use of the Bible in social and moral questions this would be an inexcusable procedure. However, what is being attempted here is representative rather than comprehensive. The aim of the previous chapter was to reach the point at which the moral teaching of the Bible, in particular of the Old Testament, had been rescued from its interpretation in mainly allegorical terms, and had been anchored in a general theory of morality. Further, the jump from Aquinas to Luther has the advantage of seeing where they agreed and differed.

We can begin immediately with the agreements. Luther was not a systematic thinker or writer like Aquinas, and his views have to be garnered from scattered sources (see Bornkamm, 1948: 103–51). He was at one with the view that whatever was worthy of praise or imitation in the Old Testament law owed these things not to the fact that they were in the Bible, but to their being instances of the fundamental principles of the natural law. Luther agreed with Aquinas that God's creative work ensured that the fundamental principles of natural law were inscribed in the hearts of human kind, even if by obstinacy or received custom the ability of human kind to discern these principles had been perverted. The law given through Moses and especially the Ten Commandments were God's method of re-stating what ought to have been known, and what had once been known.

Luther's way of making these points, however, was different from that of Aquinas; and because of the situation in which he found himself. The Reformation had spawned preachers who argued that only what was explicitly mentioned in the Bible was allowable in the Church. We shall meet similar preachers in the English Puritan Reformation. The vehemence of Luther's language owes something to the fact that he was fighting on two fronts: against what he believed to be the errors of the Roman Church, and what he believed to be the excesses of some of the Reformers.

Luther gave short shrift to the idea that the Ten Commandments might make a claim upon Christians. Noting their introduction: "I am the LORD your God who brought you out of the land of Egypt" (Exod. 20:2), Luther protested that he had not been brought out of the land of Egypt; also, that honouring his parents would not enable him to enjoy long days in the land which God had given to the ancient Israelites (Bornkamm, 1948: 108–109; referring to Luther's *Eine Unterrichtung, wie sich die Christen in Mosen sollen schicken*). The flavour of his protestations can be felt from the following quotation:

> We do not want to have Moses any longer as a rule or law-giver; and God himself does not want this state of affairs. Moses was a mediator to and law-giver to the Jewish people alone, and it is to them that he gave the law. The mouths of the gang leaders should be silenced who say "thus says Moses," "it is written in Moses" and so on. Reply "Moses has nothing to do with us." If I follow Moses in one commandment I must follow the whole of Moses. It would follow that if I took Moses for my master and law-giver, I would have to be circumcised, wash clothes according to Jewish custom, and eat and drink, dress and conduct myself in the way that Jews are commanded in the law. So we shall not hold to or accept Moses. Moses is dead. Since the coming of Christ his rule is ended (*Eine Unterricht*; my translation).

However, Moses was not, in another sense, dead but the arch-enemy of Christ! This astonishing idea takes us to the heart of Luther's theological reasons for approaching the Old Testament law as he did. "Christ is the end of the law," wrote Paul in Romans 10:4, and whatever Paul may have meant by this, Luther took him to mean that no law whatsoever, whether that of Moses or the natural law, had any role to play in the justification of humankind before God. Such justification could only depend upon the faith which God made possible through the work of Christ. This faith was, however, always in danger of being nullified by the belief that works still had to be performed in order to please God. The view that God expected Christians to obey the laws contained in the Bible because he had commanded them was one such manifestation of the way in which faith could be subverted, and explains Luther's almost shocking characterization of Moses not "as the harmless preacher of an obsolete understanding of God, but as the arch-enemy (*Todfeind*) of Christ" (Bornkamm, 1948: 122). If Moses had any useful function within a Christian economy it was as the office-holder of sin and death – as the one who displayed the connection between sin and the power of death and who in this way provided a warning to humankind not to follow the path of good works. If the Gospel contained one commandment, it was to say farewell to commandments! (Bornkamm, 1948: 124).

Along with this absolute rejection of the idea that the laws contained in the Old Testament could have any claim upon Christians at all, a great respect can also be found in Luther for some of them, especially those concerned with social justice. Also, in dealing with marriage, Luther appealed directly, and, as we shall see, radically, to laws in Leviticus 18; and his Greater Catechism contained an exposition of the Ten Commandments. Something of this will be illustrated shortly. But it must be emphasized as strongly as possible that if Luther admired parts of the Old Testament legislation and even thought that they could profitably be applied to the society of his day, this was not because they were in the Bible or commanded by Moses. It was because they were good in themselves, and were accepted freely by a Christian, in the spirit of freedom which God had granted to Christians. Christians were free to adopt parts of the Mosaic legislation and equally free to reject them (Bornkamm, 1948: 121). Luther's observation on the Sabbath commandment is interesting here.

Luther holds that the need for humans and animals to have a rest day from time to time is a dictate primarily of nature. Moses expressed this in terms of the Sabbath, which Christ also observed. However, if the issue is simply that of rest, and this is not needed in a particular case, then there is no need to observe the Sabbath; another day can be chosen, as nature indicates. To observe Sunday as a day on which to hear the preaching of God's word is another matter, and nothing to do with the Sabbath commandment to rest (see Bornkamm, 1948: 113 and note 2).

In a sermon on marriage preached in Wittenberg in 1522, Luther drew upon Leviticus 18:6–13 in order to specify the persons whom God had forbidden a man to marry, namely, his mother, stepmother, sister, stepsister, his child's daughter or stepdaughter, his father's or his mother's sister. He concluded that God did not calculate these matters in the way that lawyers did, by degrees of relationship, but by naming specific persons. This was indicated by the fact that the sister of a man's father (i.e., his aunt) was forbidden to him in marriage while his brother's daughter (i.e., his niece) was not mentioned, even though they were both related to him in the same degree (Luther, 1962: 23). These were matters concerned with consanguinity (blood relationships). On the matter of affinity (relationships established through marriage), Luther argued that only the following were forbidden: marriage with the wife of a brother of a man's father (his aunt-in-law), his daughter-in-law, his sister-in-law (his brother's wife), his stepdaughter, the child of his stepson or stepdaughter, and his wife's sister during his wife's lifetime (Lev. 18:14–18). Any person not included in the above list could lawfully be married, and this included the sister of a man's deceased wife – a relationship which the Church of England considered to be forbidden by the law of God until after the Second World War! Luther further drew attention to the Old Testament institution of levirate marriage, which required a brother-in-law (Latin, *levir*) to marry his sister-in-law (his brother's wife) if the latter was widowed and childless, the purpose being to provide the deceased brother with an heir (Deut. 25:5–9). While this provision was no longer commanded, neither was it forbidden; that is to say, a Christian who was so moved could lawfully provide children for his sister-in-law in this surrogate manner. Luther's main target in all this was the practice of the Roman Catholic Church of his day which prohibited marriage between many more relatives than those specifically named in Leviticus 18, but which was prepared to dispense such prohibitions in certain cases. Such dispensations cost money to procure, and Luther was scathing about what seemed to him to be an indefensible racket.

The sermon on marriage also contained advice on divorce; and again Luther's opinions were radical in comparison with what many conservative evangelical Christians believe today. Commenting on Matthew 19:9, "whoever divorces his wife, except for unchastity, and marries another, commits adultery," Luther declared that Christ was making it quite clear that an innocent person could divorce an adulterous spouse and could subsequently remarry. However, such procedures needed to be subject to the investigation and scrutiny of the civil authorities, or of the Christian congregation if the civil authorities declined to act. Luther was also of the opinion that civil authorities ought to put to death those found guilty of adultery, and he cited Deuteronomy 22:22–24 in support of this. If the civil authority failed to do this, the adulterer could best flee to a far country and there remarry, if unable to remain continent. There was also the possibility of reconciliation of the spouses, provided that the guilty party was publicly rebuked and caused to make amends according to the gospel (Luther, 1962: 30–33).

On the face of it, there seems to be an enormous inconsistency in Luther's use of the Bible in moral issues. The examples quoted above of his opinions on marriage and divorce seem to indicate a use of the Bible that is no different from that of modern biblical literalists, even if Luther's interpretations may have differed from theirs. There appears to be an appeal to the Bible as containing God's law. This is especially apparent in the matter of prohibited degrees of marriage, where Luther uses the Bible to reject the accumulated teachings of canon law on the subject.

It was pointed out at the beginning that Luther was not a systematic thinker or writer. Also, the turmoil produced by the Reformation required decisions to be made on many aspects of ecclesiastical and social practice for which there was often no precedent (see Bornkamm, 1983). Luther could not start with a blank page and work everything out from scratch. Further, because for him the Bible was the place in which the Gospel was revealed, it had to be held in the highest regard. In fact, it is the word "Gospel" that provides the clue to Luther's practical use of the Bible. His discovery of the justifying mercy of God in Christ and the freedom that that brought with it became the touchstone by which everything else was judged. Anything that jeopardized that freedom, especially by imposing or re-imposing any kind of law that Christians were required to observe – with the exception of the command to love God with one's whole being – was rejected in the sharpest possible tones. Luther's greatness and importance lies in the way in which his view of the gospel came to shape all his thinking and use of the Bible.

In the sermon referred to here at the beginning of this section, *Eine Unterrichtung*, Luther spoke the following words which can serve as a conclusion. Answering the rhetorical question why he preaches Moses when Moses had nothing to do with Christians, he replied:

> I shall hold to Moses and not put him under the pew, because I find in Moses some things that can also be useful for us. First of all, the commandments given to the people of Israel, that concern external existence I let go. They neither compel nor convince me. These laws are dead and obsolete, except insofar as I accept them gladly and willingly from Moses, as when I say: thus did Moses rule. I think well, so I shall follow him in this or that instance. I could also wish that rulers ruled according to the example of Moses, and if I were emperor, I would take from him an example for the laws. Not that Moses would compel me, but that I would be free to imitate him and rule in such a way.

2. *Calvin*

Calvin's understanding and use of the Old Testament law was very different from that of Luther, and it was his more affirmative approach that shaped the Reformed tradition down to conservative evangelicals of today. Calvin used the term "law" in several ways. On the one hand he meant by it "not only the Ten Commandments, which contain a complete rule of life, but the whole system of religion delivered by the hand of Moses" (Calvin,

Institutes 2.7.1). This system of religion had brought salvation through Christ to the believers under the Old Covenant, even though the latter did not know Christ explicitly. This was because the two Covenants were not contradictory but complementary. Both depended upon the mercy and graciousness of God and while the New Covenant was superior to the Old, the difference between them was a matter of administration rather than substance. Compared with that of Luther, Calvin's treatment of the relationship between the two Testaments was by way of harmony rather than radical dialectic. Calvin also understood by "law" the moral, ceremonial and political injunctions of the Old Testament, of which this second category, the ceremonial commandments, had been abrogated by the coming of Christ so far as their observance was concerned, but whose veiled significance as pointing to the work of Christ was not affected (*Institutes* 2.7.16). Paul's comments on the law, which had led Luther to his radical view of rejection, were understood differently by Calvin. Speaking of the moral law (the moral commandments of the Old Testament) Calvin cited Old Testament passages such as Psalm 19:7 – "the law of the Lord is perfect, converting the soul" – Psalm 119:105 – "thy word is a lamp unto my feet, and a light unto my path" – in order to show the importance of the law, and argued that Paul's remarks about the abrogation of the law (in passages such as Rom. 10:4 – "Christ is the end of the law" – and Gal. 3:24 – "the law was our schoolmaster to bring us to Christ") did not apply to the (moral) law itself but to "its power of constraining the conscience" (*Institutes* 2.7.15). By this Calvin meant that Christians were free from the demands of a law that required rigid and exact observance and left no deviation, however small, unpunished. But if Christians were free from this legal tyranny over human conscience, it remained true that the law had lost none of its authority and had to be accorded the same respect and obedience as had always been the case (*Institutes* 2.7.15).

Granted these views, it is no surprise that Calvin regarded the so-called third use of the law (the other uses being to make clear the righteous demands of God and to restrain vice by the threat of punishment) as its principal use. Calvin acknowledged that for Christians, the law was written on their hearts by the finger of God. This did not, however, mean that they possessed all moral wisdom and lived lives accordingly. Christians needed to meditate on the law so as to be drawn away from the slippery paths of sin and to be drawn towards the wisdom and purity contained in it. Whether or not Calvin had Luther in mind when he wrote that "Some unskilful persons, from not attending to this boldly discard the whole law of Moses, and do away with both its Tables, imagining it unchristian to adhere to a doctrine which contains the ministration of death" (*Institutes* 2.7.13), the passage indicates the gulf between Luther and Calvin in this matter.

Calvin's expositions of the moral law are contained in his *Institutes of the Christian Religion* (of which the final edition appeared in 1559) and his commentary on Exodus, the *Mosaica*, which was written or dictated beginning in 1559 (Parker, 1986: 32). In fact, the *Mosaica* consisted of a commentary on the book of Exodus up to chapter 19, after which the Ten Commandments of Exodus 20 were used as the basis for expounding laws from other parts of the Pentateuch which Calvin held to be connected with or illustrative of individual clauses of the Ten Commandments (see Parker, 1986: 122–75). In what follows, the material in the *Institutes* will be dealt with first.

A small preliminary point is that Calvin divided the Ten Commandments so as to make the first one the injunction to have no gods but the Lord, the second to be the prohibition against graven images and the third to be the injunction against taking the Lord's name in vain. This division went against that usually accepted (also to this day) in the Catholic and Lutheran Churches and in Judaism, and became the basis for what is generally accept in English-speaking Protestantism (including the Anglican Church).

The most striking thing about Calvin's exposition is that he turned the negative form of the eight commandments that begin "thou shalt not..." into positive assertions. Thus, "thou shalt not take the name of the Lord thy God in vain," is initially summarized as "the majesty of the name of God is to be held sacred" (*Institutes* 2.8.22). Likewise, "thou shalt not commit adultery" is summarized as because "God loves chastity and purity, we ought to guard against all uncleanness" (*Institutes* 2.8.41). This tactic of expressing negative commandments as positive principles then opens the way for Calvin to write generally about the positive principles that have been enunciated. For example, "thou shall not steal" being positively summarized as "injustice being an abomination to God, we must render to every man his due" becomes the occasion for comments on any type of fraud or dishonest dealing, on the need for Christians to be content with their lot and to pay due deference to the authority of rulers. At the same time, rulers are urged to protect the public peace, to protect the good and curb the bad. Ministers of churches are exhorted to exercise their ministries sincerely and honestly and to be good shepherds of their flocks. Parents, children and servants are exhorted to pay due regard to those to whom honour can legitimately be expected (*Institutes* 2.8.45–46). All this is a far cry from "thou shalt not steal" but representative of Calvin's method. "Thou shalt not kill" is summarized as "the safety of all ought to be considered as entrusted to each," and leads to comments on avoiding all forms of violence, being vigilant in warding off harm, and assisting in removing danger (*Institutes* 2.8.39). What emerges from the exposition is that this is not a *legalistic* interpretation of the commandments. The principles that the commandments are held to enshrine govern every facet of Christian life before God. Taken together, they describe a way of living that God has made possible and to which Christians must aspire. This is preaching rather than legislation.

It is in this spirit that Calvin deals with the commandment about observing the Sabbath day, and his treatment is in sharp contrast to the sabbatarianism that was later to develop in churches claiming to be "Calvinist." He begins by recognizing the prominence of this commandment in the Bible: "there is no commandment the observance of which the Almighty more strictly enforces" (*Institutes* 2.8.29). Also, by stating that God rested from the work of creation on the Sabbath, Moses indicates that the Sabbath rest is an imitation of the Creator (*Institutes* 2.8.30). Yet Calvin has no doubt "that on the advent of our Lord Jesus Christ, the ceremonial part of the commandment was abolished" (*Institutes* 2.8.31).

Did this mean that the *moral* part of the commandment remained, the observance of one day in seven? By no means! Calvin sharply criticized those who changed the day but mentally ascribed to it the same sanctity as the Jews did to the Sabbath. This was to indulge in superstition, and was open to the rebukes found at Isaiah 1:13 and 58:13. On the other hand, it was necessary for Christians to meet together on stated days for worship, prayer, and hearing the word of God just as it was also important for there to be stated days when servants and labourers could rest. Calvin did not object to this "stated day" being Sunday as long as this was not done as a *religious* observance.

As was mentioned earlier, from chapter 20 of the commentary on Exodus, Calvin used each of the Ten Commandments as an occasion for bringing together and commenting on all those other parts of the Pentateuch that seemed to him to fall under the scope of a particular commandment. Thus the treatment of the first commandment, of having no God but the Lord, includes discussions of Deuteronomy 18:9–14 (the prohibition of various forms of divination and sorcery), Deuteronomy 13:1–4 (false prophets) and Leviticus 18:21 (prohibiting the sacrifice of children to Molech). There follows a Ceremonial Appendix which deals, among other things, with the observance of the Passover; the consecration of first-born children and animals; the payments of tribute (in Exod. 30:11–16 where Moses is commanded to levy half a shekel on all those aged twenty and above when a census of the people is taken); the offering of first fruits and the purification of women after childbirth. There is also a Judicial Appendix which deals with penalties which are liable to be imposed upon those who fail to carry out the requirements of the first commandment. All in all, this part of the commentary on Exodus amounts to an exhaustive discussion of the legal parts of the Pentateuch, seen as the work of Moses, but reorganized by Calvin into a systematic whole.

Much of the commentary explains the laws in their historical context in the life of ancient Israel, with little resort to allegory. An exception is Calvin's treatment of clean and unclean animals where, appealing to a long tradition of allegorical interpretation of these regulations (Parker, 1986: 149), cleaving the hoof is taken to refer to "dividing" the mysteries of Scripture and chewing the cud to meditation upon heavenly teaching. Calvin's adherence to the distinction between ceremonial and moral laws, of which the former were not binding upon Christians, obviated the need for discussing the relevance of the former for Calvin's times. However, the distinction between ceremonial and moral laws was not always easy to draw, especially in the case of penalties, whose administration in any case was a matter for civil and not ecclesiastical authorities. On the question of the penalties enjoined in the Old Testament for breaches of the first commandment, Calvin distinguished between the *substance* of the commandment and their *form* (Parker, 1986: 151), with the latter being practices that were relevant only to ancient Israel. However, it was possible for the *substance* of the commanded penalties to be relevant for Christians; and if the laws of the civil authorities prescribed even the death penalty for teachings that undermined the true understanding and worship of God, then this could legitimately be carried out. Parker (1986: 152) notes the problem of knowing precisely which Old Testament penalties Calvin believed still to have force in a Christian state. He suggests that Calvin took some political laws in the Old Testament to have continuing force, and others not. He notes the further problem that it was not easy to know whether, when speaking of an enforceable civil law, Calvin was referring to the Old Testament, to a mediaeval interpretation of it, or to a secular mediaeval law that was identical with an Old Testament law. This is an important observation, because otherwise it might be possible to conclude that Calvin's application of aspects of the Old Testament law to Christians of his day was more literal and extensive than might have been the case. That his discussions of the matter were subtle and nuanced has been indicated above. Many who seemingly followed in his footsteps lacked Calvin's subtlety.

Chapter 7

THE SIXTEENTH AND SEVENTEENTH CENTURIES

1. *Richard Hooker (1554–1600)*

Hooker's *Of the Laws of Ecclesiastical Polity* contains a remarkable, and seemingly very modern, view of how the Bible should be used. He began work on the *Laws* in 1591, of which the preface and first four books were published in 1593 and book five in 1597. The remaining books (six to eight) which were apparently in draft rather than final form, did not appear until 1648 (books six and eight) and 1661 (book seven). Their content is the more remarkable given the circumstances in which the work was written.

The accession of Elizabeth I in 1558 to the English throne gave hope to many returning exiles that the Reformation begun under Henry VIII and Edward VI could now be completed. Many of the exiles had found refuge in centres of Reformed theology such as Geneva, Zurich, Basel and Strasbourg. In some cases they had ministered to English-speaking exile congregations, using forms of worship based upon usage in Geneva, rather than on the 1552 Book of Common Prayer. When they discovered that Elizabeth intended to maintain something like the situation that had obtained in the reign of Edward VI, the exiles were bitterly disappointed.

The opposition to the regime established under Archbishop Matthew Parker took several forms as it developed in the years leading up to Hooker's work (see Collinson, 1967). For some, the notion of a bishop was not necessarily unacceptable, provided that the office was seen as one of administration, and not of necessity. Calvin, after all, had identified bishop, priest, pastor and minister as one office (Collinson, 1967: 104), and as long as they were thought of as superintendents, bishops were not objectionable to Reformed churches. However, under Elizabeth, bishops were expected to enforce the royal supremacy over the Church of England. They were to function not constitutionally, as superintendents acting in consultation with other ministers and congregations, but monarchically, ruling over the "inferior" clergy and their parishes. When, in 1565, the bishops took steps to enforce the wearing of the surplice and certain items of dress in public by the clergy, former exiles and others who hoped for a more "Genevan" style of Reformation in England were deeply distressed.

A more radical form of opposition to Elizabeth and her bishops took the view that the government of the Church of England was contrary to that implied in and demanded by the Bible. Supporters of this movement wanted nothing less than the introduction of a Presbyterian form of government of the church, and the replacement of the Book of Common Prayer, (with its commitment to episcopacy) by a liturgy based upon that of Geneva. To this end, attempts were made in 1584–86 to compile and to have approved by Parliament, a Book of Discipline that would replace episcopacy with Presbyterian forms of synodical government and would authorize the use of the Geneva liturgy (Collinson, 1967: 291–308).

There is no need here to discuss the outcome of the attempt to get parliamentary approval for the Book of Discipline, of which Collinson has observed that "the programme contained in the bill and book was so extreme, so manifestly unacceptable, not merely to the Queen but to all responsible opinion, that one both marvels at the sanguinity of its sponsors, and speculates as to the precise place of these parliamentary manoeuvres in their total strategy" (Collinson, 1967: 317). The important point for the present section is that when Hooker was appointed as Master of the Temple in 1585, he had to share the church with Walter Travers who, if not the author of the Book of Discipline, was probably involved in its production. Since 1581 Travers had held the post of afternoon lecturer at the Temple. In 1585–86, a parallel course of lectures at the Temple by Travers and Hooker set out conflicting views about ecclesiastical polity.

Underlying the differences between the supporters of Presbyterian forms and upholders of the status quo was the question of the Bible, its authority, and how it should be used, and it was to this debate that Hooker made a contribution which has much of value even for today.

The main line of argument of Hooker's opponents, according to Hooker's exposition of the matter (in *Laws*, 3, ch. 8), was that the laws and customs which governed the organization of the Church of England were based upon human reason, and that human reason was flawed and fallible. The opponents based this verdict upon the following arguments. First, the "natural man" could not perceive the things of God; they could only be perceived spiritually (1 Cor. 2:14). Second, Paul explicitly warned against philosophy in Colossians 2:8. Third, heretics had always been great admirers of human wisdom and secular learning and it was their advancement of these things above obedience to Christian truth that had enabled them to lead themselves and others astray. Fourth, Paul in 1 Corinthians 1:19 had quoted the following words from the Old Testament "I will destroy the wisdom of the wise, and will cast away the understanding of the prudent" (Isa. 29:19). Fifth, whereas the word of God was a two-edged sword (cp. Heb. 4:12) human reason was like the armour of Saul when tried by the youthful David – cumbersome. Paul had asserted that his preaching had "not been in the enticing speech of man's wisdom, but in plain evidence of the Spirit and of power" (1 Cor. 2:4). Sixth, a person's faith in the Gospel was not something that resulted from reason. It was the result of the work of the Spirit of God in a person's heart. Hooker summed up the position of his opponents in words whose import can still be heard today, whether in condemnation of biblical scholarship or in commending the virtues of "simple" faith: "an opinion hath spread itself very far in the world, as if the way to be ripe in faith were to be raw in wit and judgement; as if reason were an enemy with religion, childish simplicity the mother of ghostly and divine wisdom" (*Laws*, 3, ch. 8: 4).

In reply to these points Hooker objected that terms such as "human reason" were being used in too crude a fashion. While it was true that certain aspects of Christian faith could not be grasped by reason (Hooker gives as an example the Roman governor Festus, who took Paul's preaching about Christ's death and resurrection to be a sign of madness in Acts 26:24), it was clear from Romans 1:21 and 32 that the light of human reason could and did lead humankind in general to know how God intended them to live. They could not plead ignorance of God's laws even if the latter had not been specially revealed to them. Second, Paul's warning against philosophy in Colossians was not a warning against philosophy as such, but against a variety and use of it which sought to make unreasonable things seem reasonable and attractive. Third, while it was true that some philosophers had been "very unsound in belief," some believers had been great philosophers. Here, Hooker argued that the refutation of heresy required precisely the kind of deployment of reason that his opponents wished to discredit, and he referred to Augustine and Tertullian as exponents of reason to this end. Fourth, it was necessary to distinguish between human knowledge which could be universally recognized as expressing truth or wisdom, whatever the source of this knowledge, and the misuse of reason so that people became disputers for their own sake, rather than in order to establish what was true. As examples of the first category, Hooker cited the mathematical wisdom of the Chaldeans (Babylonians) or the "rational and oratorial wisdom of the Grecians." To deny the dignity of these and similar examples of human wisdom was to impugn God himself, who was the source of these sparks of enlightenment.

Hooker's fifth and sixth arguments are longer and more involved than the preceding ones and touch on some fundamental points. He begins by maintaining (in regard to the passages from Heb. 4:12 about the word of God being a two-edged sword) that the exercise of reason is itself an inescapable part of the interpretation of the Bible: "we do not add reason as a supplement of any maim or defect therein [i.e., Scripture], but as a necessary instrument, without which we could not reap by the Scripture's perfection that fruit and benefit which it yieldeth" (*Laws*, 3, ch. 8: 10). But if this was true why did Paul maintain that his preaching had "not been in the persuasive speeches of human wisdom, but in demonstration of the Spirit and of power" (1 Cor. 2:4)? Hooker distinguished the twelve Apostles ("twelve simple and unlearned men") from Paul. The former had been supernaturally endowed by God with the power of utterance, so that those who heard them and knew them to be unlearned would be the more attentive to their preaching. It was otherwise with Paul. But the fact that he had not been a disciple of Christ was used against him by those who sought to deny his authority. This was why he adamantly argued that his preaching depended for its effectiveness not upon the fact that he was a learned and educated man, but upon the work of God's Spirit.

Hooker next turns to the question of how it is that we know, or come to believe, that Scripture contains all the supernaturally revealed truth that is necessary for salvation. His account is honest and realistic. It begins with tradition, that is, what is received from one's forebears and from the authority of the Church. But this is not a passive and mindless acceptance: "the more we bestow our labour in reading or hearing the mysteries thereof, the more we find that the thing itself [i.e., Scripture] doth answer our received opinion concerning it" (*Laws*, 3, ch. 8: 14). This is the position of a believer; but what of unbelievers? Hooker argues that the "ancient Fathers" sought to defend their beliefs about the authority of Scripture by recourse to proofs and arguments that they hoped would convince unbelievers. Further, reason not only helped to confirm believers in the truth of their belief, it was a standard tool in any disputation with unbelievers. Hooker further backed his defence of the importance of reason by giving examples of its use in the Bible. Thus Peter called upon his readers to render "a reason of their belief" (1 Pet. 3:15), while Jesus in the Gospels disputed with the Pharisees as to whether Christ was the son of David (Matt. 22:41–46).

At the end of considering the arguments against using reason in order to regulate the affairs of the Church of England, Hooker was able to enquire "whether the light of reason be so pernicious, that in devising laws for the Church men ought not by it to search what may be fit and convenient" (*Laws*, 3, ch. 8: 18).

The section dealing with a defence of reason is preceded by one which discusses the purpose of Scripture, and whether matters of discipline (i.e., church order) are different from matters of faith and salvation. Hooker argues that there is such a distinction (between discipline, and faith and salvation) and makes a further distinction between what is *commanded* in the word (the Bible) and what is *grounded* upon the word. This latter distinction is clarified with regard to Paul's advice about marriage in 1 Corinthians 7:8, 26. This advice is that it is better for the unmarried and widows to stay unmarried. While this goes against much that is presumed in the Bible, namely, that people should marry, there is no commandment to the effect that they should, so that Paul's advice does not amount to a breach of any commandment. Those who follow Paul's advice and do not marry are *grounding* their action upon the word rather than being *commanded* by it. The implication of Hooker's argument appears to be that what the New Testament says about church order and discipline has the same status as Paul's advice about not getting married. It is something that can be followed or not followed as people decide for themselves. Those who decided not to follow the advice are not breaking any commandment, and they are certainly not being disobedient to the word (the Bible) if they espouse a system of church order that has developed over the centuries forms that do not correspond to those in the New Testament.

It is different with matters that touch upon faith and salvation. What the Bible teaches on these matters must be believed, and the Bible contains all things that are needful to be believed for salvation. Other matters, called accessories, are likened by Hooker to a path that may be faced with grass, with gravel or with stone, but which remains the same path however it is faced. For the distinction between things that are *necessary* and those that are *accessories* Hooker appeals to the teaching of Jesus, and his condemnation of the Pharisees in Matthew 23:23 for ignoring the weightier matters of the law, that is, justice, mercy and faith, in favour of attention to more trivial matters.

Diarmaid MacCulloch has remarked (MacCulloch, 2003: 506) that while Hooker's *Laws* made little impact in their day, later readers came increasingly to recognize that his arguments

> combated the whole mindset behind the sermon-based "Bible alone" style of English Reformed Protestantism, let alone the argument for a Presbyterian future for the English Church... Central to his argument was a careful

sifting of the ways in which scripture should be used as an authority for Christian life and practice, and the ways in which it should not. The purpose was to widen the areas which could be regarded as matters indifferent, *adiaphora*. These might then be considered using a variety of norms, and so they were open to the authorities of Church and Commonwealth to regulate in the wider public interest.

The fact that Hooker's *Laws* had little effect on how the Bible was used in his time is unimportant in the present work, which is meant to be illustrative, and not a history of the Bible's use. The value of Hooker is that his approach was "modern" in the sense that it restricted the authority of the Bible to matters of faith and salvation, allowed for the importance of traditions handed down over the centuries, and emphasized that human reason and wisdom, far from being enemies of things spiritual, were necessary tools for the interpretation and understanding of the Bible itself. Hooker is an important witness to the diversity of approaches to the Bible long before the rise of modern biblical criticism. He gives the lie to any attempt to argue that Christians have always applied the Bible to every aspect of Christian life and practice, and that modern approaches which deny its applicability to many areas of modern life are fateful consequences of "liberalism" and biblical criticism. Yet even in such a staunch defender of Reformed theology as Richard Baxter, who worked a century later than Hooker we find a use of reason and judgement in applying the Bible to the concerns of his day that is far more discriminating than "conservative" efforts of today.

2. Richard Baxter (1615–1691)

One of the most important compendia on the Christian life was completed by Richard Baxter in 1664–65 and published in 1673. Entitled *A Christian Directory* it ran to almost a thousand pages and was distinguished not only by its thoroughness, but by an enormous breadth of learning, as can be seen from the section in which Baxter described the kind of library that a Minister of the Gospel should have at his disposal (Baxter, 2000: 732–36). Even his 'poorest library' (Baxter, 2000: 732) embraced scores of titles covering the Fathers, works of theology, commentaries and lexicons. The work's "reformed" tenor is indicated by the inclusion of the Reformed Liturgy for Sunday services, orders for Holy Communion and Baptism, and "occasional offices" such as Matrimony. Yet the author was offered and declined, the bishopric of Hereford after the Declaration of Charles II.

Baxter was educated privately, and ordained in 1638 by the Bishop of Worcester in order to become a teacher at a free school in Dudley. In 1641 he became Minister in Kidderminster Parish Church, the Vicar retaining the living and vicarage but remaining inactive. Uncertain about whom to support in the Civil War, he eventually became Chaplain to a regiment on the Roundhead side (i.e., that opposed to Charles I) but opposed Cromwell when the latter gained the ascendancy. From the Restoration of the monarchy (1660) to the Act of Uniformity (1662), which required worship to be according to the Book of Common Prayer, Baxter preached in various London churches. Unable to accept the Act of Uniformity he retired to Acton to write, producing *A Christian Directory* among other things. The Indulgence of 1672 enabled him to resume preaching in London but the Oxford Act led to his imprisonment and the seizure of his property (1682–85). James II (1685) reversed some of these policies and the "revolution" which brought William and Mary to the throne (1688) brought much relief. Baxter was able to enjoy some last years of preaching and lecturing. The turbulent years through which he lived gave him more than ample scope to consider how Christians should frame their lives, and in accordance with biblical teaching.

Baxter's importance lies in the fact that he was totally committed to the Bible as the infallible word of God. Yet at the same time, and without any embarrassment, he made distinctions and concessions that today would be regarded as evidence of "liberal" tendencies in some conservative evangelical quarters. Consider, for example, his answer to the question "May one be saved who believeth that the Scripture hath any mistake or error, and believeth it not all?" (Baxter, 2000: 724). Baxter allows that a person who does not accept Jude, 2 Peter, 2 John, 3 John and Revelation as canonical or the word of God can be saved "so he heartily believe the rest, or the essentials." The same would be the case for anyone who held that the Bible's infallibility did not extend "to an infallibility in every by-expression, phrase, citation or circumstance." The following section, in which Baxter defines those who "give too much" to Scripture, criticizes those who "feign it to be instead of all grammars, logic, philosophy, and all other arts and sciences, and to be a lawyer, physician, mariner, architect, husbandman, and tradesman, to do his work by." As touching upon church order, Baxter criticizes those who hold that only those things that are mentioned in the Bible may be observed "as time, place, vesture, gesture, utensils, methods, words." Of particular interest from the point of view of biblical criticism is Baxter's criticism of those "that say that God hath so preserved the Scripture, as that there are no various readings and doubtful texts thereupon [here he referred readers to the *Critica sacra* of Ludwig Cappellus (1650)], and that no written or printed copes have been corrupted (when Dr Heylin tells us, that the King's printer printed the seventh commandment, Thou shalt commit adultery)" (Baxter, 2000: 725). This latter reference was to the so-called "Wicked Bible," an edition of the Authorized Version published in 1631 by the King's printer, Barker, which omitted the all-important "not." Still on the subject of biblical criticism, Baxter's views on the canon were remarkably forward-looking. "It is not of necessity to salvation to believe every book or verse in Scripture, to be canonical, or written by the Spirit of God" he affirmed (Baxter, 2000: 712), and he went on to say that if the Protestant canon proved to be defective in any one book, this would not affect the Bible's role in mediating saving faith. There is nothing here of the "either you have to accept everything or you can trust nothing" type of argument still advanced today against critical biblical scholarship. Baxter was fully aware of the historical circumstances involved in the growth of the Bible to its canonical forms and could allow that "if some book be lost, (as Enoch's prophecy, or Paul's epistle to the Laodiceans [see Col. 4:16], or any other of his epistles not named in the rest), or if any hereafter should be lost or doubted of, as the Canticles, or the second or third epistles of John, the epistle of Jude, etc., it would not follow, that all true faith and hope of salvation were lost with it" (Baxter, 2000: 712).

Baxter's views on actual practice were consistent with his theory. Because he held that gestures and postures assumed in worship were to be regulated by custom and common sense, he was prepared to bow at the name of Jesus if he was a member of a church where this was customary (Baxter, 2000: 686). With regard to applying the Bible too literally to practical matters, Baxter distinguished "universal laws" from those in the Bible that were "local, personal, or alterable" (Baxter, 2000: 557). In illustration of this he continued "If you should mistake all the Jewish laws for universal laws...into how many errors it would lead you... Every man is not to abstain from vineyards and wine as the Rechabites were [cp. Jer. 35:2–10]; nor every man to go forth to preach in the garb as Christ sent the twelve and seventy disciples; nor every man to administer or receive the Lord's supper in an upper room of a house, in the evening, with eleven or twelve only." It was necessary to recognize that some customs were appropriate to some lands and not to others. Baptism by immersion was appropriate in a warm country but not in a cold one. Regarding the comment in 1 Corinthians 11:10 about women covering their heads, Baxter allowed that "in some places, where long hair or covering may have a contrary significance, the case may be contrary" (Baxter, 2000: 558).

In answer to the question "Is not the law of Moses abrogated, and the whole Old Testament out of date, and therefore not to be read publicly and preached on?" (Baxter, 2000: 719) Baxter argued that the law of nature was the law of Christ and that this law was "much expounded" in the Old Testament. This law amounted to a "covenant of grace" made with Adam and Noah for all mankind and to that extent was still valid. The law of Moses was valid and binding in so far as it articulated natural law. In its particularity as concerned with the laws of a nation, it was not binding. "Even the Decalogue itself was to them [the Jews] a political law" (Baxter, 2000: 719). How was all this applied to particular cases? What follows can only be a tiny selection from a massive and comprehensive work.

1. *Degrees of Marriage (Baxter, 2000: 404)*
"The law of Moses is not in force to us," but if Leviticus 18 has force, it is because it expresses "God's exposition of his own law of nature." If the laws of a country permit marriage within closer relationships than allowed in Leviticus 18, the stipulations of Leviticus must nevertheless be obeyed – but not simply because they are in the Bible. Baxter notes that Adam's sons lawfully married their sisters and agrees that such marriages would be appropriate today for a brother and sister "cast alone upon a foreign wilderness" (Baxter, 2000: 405).

2. *Divorce and Remarriage (Baxter, 2000: 445–47)*
Baxter allowed that either party could divorce the other on the grounds of adultery. While recognizing that Matthew 5:31 and 19:9 spoke only of a *man* divorcing his *wife* on the grounds of adultery, he knew "no reason to blame those countries, whose laws allow the wife to sue out of a divorce, as well as the husband." On the vexed subject of the remarriage of divorced persons, something that conservative evangelicals in Britain hold to be forbidden by biblical teaching, Baxter considered the implications of Matthew 5:31–32 which says that remarriage with a divorced woman brings about adultery. He inclined to the view that where a woman was the innocent party in a divorce, and the remarriage of her husband put an end to any hope of reconciliation, a remarriage of the innocent person to another was not unlawful.

3. *Slavery*
This institution, never formally condemned in the Bible, was nonetheless dealt with in a sensitive matter by Baxter. His starting point was that loss of a person's liberty was admissible only as a punishment for crime. Brotherly

love made obligatory the guarantee of a person's freedom in the absence of due punishment. This enabled Baxter to condemn in the strongest possible terms the trafficking in slaves known in his day. "To go as pirates and catch up poor negroes or people of another land, that never forfeited life or liberty, and to make them slaves, and sell them is one of the worst kinds of thieving in the world; and such persons are to be taken for the common enemies of mankind" (Baxter, 2000: 462).

4. *Usury*

To what extent Christians were bound by biblical laws that prohibited the charging of interest (e.g., Lev. 25:35–36) was a lively matter of debate in the sixteenth and seventeenth centuries. The problem enabled Baxter to state again the way in which he considered the Old Testament to be binding upon Christians. "The law of Moses, as such, is not in force," he declared (Baxter, 200: 838) citing in his defence 2 Corinthians 3:7, where the Mosaic law is described as the "ministration of death," Galatians 3:19 (the law was added because of transgressions) and Ephesians 2:15 (Christ abolished "in his flesh the enmity, even the law") among other texts. However, "so much of them [i.e., the laws of Moses] as are part of the law of nature, or of any positive law of Christ, or of the civil law of any state, are binding as they are such natural, Christian or civil laws. But not one of them as Mosaical, though the Mosaical law is of great use to help us to understand the law of nature in many particular instances, in which it is somewhat difficult to us" (Baxter, 2000: 838).

These comments on the validity of the law of Moses were addressed to the supposition, which Baxter would have contested, that the Old Testament clearly forbade lending money on interest. In his view, what was forbidden was the charging of interest that took advantage of people who found themselves in unfortunate circumstances. On Luke 6:32, 35, passages that had traditionally been taken to mean that Jesus had forbidden the charging of interest, Baxter maintained that the verses meant that one should lend to poor people even when there was little prospect that they would be in a position to repay the debt.

5. *Tithing*

Should Christians given a tenth of their income to God? Baxter's answer (Baxter, 2000: 887–92) is long and involved, taking into account many things such as the fact that in Old Testament times, in addition to tithes, there were offerings of first fruits, sacrifices, and gifts of the poor. Times and circumstances would vary. "Your proportion of the tenth part is too much for some, and much too little for others" (Baxter, 2000: 891). The duties of households towards providing for their members are fully discussed, as is the need to support the church and their ministers. Baxter is also wary of the argument that once people have tithed, they have no further responsibility for supporting the poor and giving charitably. The key texts for Baxter in this matter were 1 Corinthians 16:2 "Let every one of you lay by him in store, as God hath prospered him" and 2 Corinthians 8:12 "according to that a man hath." What these texts did was not to prescribe a law for giving, but to appeal to the hearts and conscience of Christians to respond according to the measure of their gratitude to God. On the other hand, Baxter allowed "that ordinarily a tenth part at least is requisite," the words "at least" being noteworthy.

Baxter knew the work of Hooker, and referred to it occasionally in order to refute specific points (e.g., Baxter, 2000: 745–48 on the duty of subjects to their rulers). No doubt he disagreed with Hooker's commitment to episcopacy (see Baxter, 2000: 640), but in many respects Hooker and Baxter were closer than it might appear. Both placed a high value upon secular learning and thus on the function of reason. Further, Hooker's insistence that reason was not something additional to what was revealed in the Bible, but an essential element in the interpretation and application of the Bible was surely also fundamental to Baxter's approach. If the law of Moses is binding upon Christians only to the extent that it contains the law of nature, the law of Christ, and civil laws, the question arises as to how the presence of these laws is be discerned in the law of Moses. Again, Baxter's view that some Old Testament prescriptions are universal while others are local, personal and temporary raises the question of how one decides which is which. It was all very well for Baxter to claim that "the text itself will one way or other show us, when a command or example is universally and durably obligatory, and when not" (Baxter, 2000: 712), but surely his own illustrations, not to mention the history of the use of the Bible before his time and since, provide abundant examples of the fact that the text does *not* in many cases show whether a command or example is universally and durably obligatory. The answer must surely be that it was human reason that decided which laws were universal and binding, and which were not. Of course, the human reason invoked was shaped by Christian tradition and no doubt guided by a reverence for God and an earnest desire to seek the truth. But it was also a human reason that depended upon the scientific knowledge and social conventions of the times; and as these latter things changed, so would reason's discernment of what was universal and binding in the Bible. All this is not to criticize or denigrate Baxter. On the contrary,

A Christian Directory is a monumental work of Christian scholarship of the highest standards and integrity, and it is precisely its breadth of learning, its generosity of spirit and its incisive use of human rationality that makes it, not a work than can be uncritically accepted in today's world, but a model and example of how Christian commitment and human learning can be applied to the deployment of the Bible in the face of contemporary issues.

Chapter 8

The Eighteenth and Nineteenth Centuries

1. J. D. Michaelis (1717–1791)

In 1814 an English translation of Johann David Michaelis' *Commentaries on the Laws of Moses* made available to the English-speaking public a work that stood on the dividing line between traditional and historical-critical views of the authorship of the Bible, and which situated the laws of the Pentateuch in their historical setting as never before. The German original had been published in 1770–75 and several projects to have it translated into English had foundered in the eighteenth century (Michaelis, 1814: I, xiii–xvi). One reason for their being translated was that they were the work of an eminent German Orientalist who defended the Mosaic authorship of the Pentateuch at a time (i.e., the early-nineteenth century) when this view of the Pentateuch was beginning to be assailed. Michaelis could therefore be cited as a witness in favour of the traditional position. What, however, was distinctive about Michaelis' commentaries was the fact that he had investigated the historical and social setting of the Mosaic legislation with a thoroughness that had never been attempted before and has seldom been equalled since, once account is taken of the restrictions on the knowledge then available to him.

Michaelis was one of the encyclopaedic scholars of the eighteenth century who had combed not only the classical and Arabic sources for information about the ancient world (he believed that the Arabic language and cultures had preserved customs from the very beginning of human history) but who had made an extensive study of accounts of so-called primitive peoples known to eighteenth-century Europeans. He had been the prime mover behind the scientific expedition to the Orient sponsored by the King of Denmark in 1761. But there was another side to his work that is interesting for the present study, namely, that he lived in a country where a number of Protestant rulers exercised jurisdiction over larger or smaller principalities, and where the question of the applicability of the Mosaic law to the regulation of those principalities was in some cases a burning and contentious issue.

On his own admission (Michaelis, 1814: III, 56) Michaelis' treatment of the laws of Moses was not theological, but expounded the laws "only in the light in which they would appear to a civilian or to a person philosophizing on legislative policy." Thus there are no theological arguments that appeal to the New Testament, or the considerations met, for example, in Baxter. It is, however, implicitly assumed that moral commandments may retain their authority, while civil commandments will not.

In his opening statements Michaelis makes clear his views "that God never meant them [the Pentateuchal laws] to bind any other nation but the Israelites; and that it would be quite foolish to detach particular parts from their connection with the rest, and to attempt ingrafting them on other systems, to which they must prove incongruous" (Michaelis, 1814: I, 5). This, the detaching of particular laws from their connection with the rest, is precisely what happens in much modern use of the Bible, of course. Be that as it may, the whole point of the *Commentaries* is to show, by painstaking research into the social background to the laws, that they could not possibly be directly applicable to Michaelis' world, a world so different from that of the Bible. Although our knowledge of the world of the Bible today differs considerably from that reconstructed by Michaelis, the challenge of his work has lost none of its force. There is one respect, however, in which Michaelis had not entirely distanced himself from the view that because something was in the Bible it must have some validity today, and this comes in the surprising statement that a law given by Moses cannot be sinful (Michaelis, 1814: I, 6). Referring specifically to slavery and to divorce on grounds other than adultery, Michaelis argues that because Moses allowed slavery and divorce, it would not be sinful for a ruler to permit these things. He does not advocate them, and regarded people who sought divorce on grounds other than adultery as committing a sin. It would not, however, be sinful for a ruler to permit such a divorce if it averted a greater evil. Michaelis appealed here to the concept of the hardness of heart of the people (cp. Mark 10:5), an idea that today would be understood to mean that all moral judgements have to be situated in specific circumstances, which may affect the form they take.

Michaelis acknowledged that the parts of the Mosaic law that were thought in his day to be most strongly in force were those relating to forbidden degrees of marriage, and his discussion of them will be briefly considered. According to Michaelis there were three opinions current in his day in Protestant German principalities regarding the interpretation of Leviticus 18 and 20. The first opinion was that only marriages expressly mentioned in the biblical text were forbidden. Thus, whereas marriage with an aunt is expressly prohibited (see Lev. 18:12–13 which mentions the sister of a man's father and the sister of his mother) there is no mention of a man's niece. It was therefore held that a ruler might properly allow a man to marry his niece and Michaelis claims that George II allowed such marriages in Hanover after 1755 (Michaelis, 1814: I, 43). It is noteworthy that at the time of writing this section (2005) marriage with a niece is prohibited in England and Wales. Michaelis also points out that marriage with a (deceased) wife's sister "had for a long time" been permitted in Hanover. In England such marriages became legal as a civil ceremony only in 1907 and as a church ceremony only after the Second World War.

A second, stricter, interpretation of Leviticus 18 and 20 held that it was degrees of relatedness, not individual relationships that were prohibited by the Mosaic legislation. Thus, the prohibition of marriage with an aunt also applied to marriage with a niece. This latter type of marriage seems to have been a particular problem in Hanover, because George III, who acceded in 1760, was "repeatedly solicited for dispensations" to allow it (Michaelis, 1814: II, 44). The consistory that he consulted was divided in its opinion, and eventually decided to play safe and not to allow such marriages.

A third view was that some of the prohibited marriages were *civil* regulations given to ancient Israel only and therefore allowable in today's world. The others were *moral*, and covered relationships between parents, children, brothers or sisters. It was these only that should not be permitted under any circumstances.

This brief outline has confirmed once more that using the Bible in a moral and social issue involved much more than simply applying the text to a modern situation. Other factors, in this case the question of whether Leviticus 18 and 20 referred to degrees of relatedness or to specific relationships, determined the interpretation and the application. In discussing Michaelis' *Commentaries* attention has been focused on the topic of permitted marriages because this was the area in which it was most commonly agreed that the Mosaic laws might be applicable to the society of his day. For the rest, Michaelis had no difficulty in showing that the entirely different social situations of the world of the Bible made it impossible to apply its laws to today's world, and it must be remembered that this was maintained by a scholar who believed firmly in the Mosaic, and therefore divine, origin of the Pentateuchal laws. The next development in the history of scholarship would be to deny the Mosaic origin of the laws, and thereby require a new theory to make sense of them within a general Christian understanding.

2. *The Nineteenth Century: A New Approach*

From a modern ethical standpoint the Bible, especially the Old Testament, contains material that falls far short of contemporary moral standards. This is not a new discovery. Augustine, writing in the fifth century, acknowledged that Abraham's example in fathering a child by his wife's servant was not an example that Christians could or should follow (Augustine, *City of God* 16, ch. 25 commenting on Gen. 16:1–4). Abraham had, however, acted without lust, and was thus vindicated in his particular situation. Actions such as Joshua's wholesale slaughter of the Canaanites (cp. Josh. 10:40) were defended on the grounds that the Canaanites were grievous sinners in God's sight and deserved to be punished in this way. The behaviour of David in committing adultery with Bathsheba and then arranging for her husband to be killed in battle (2 Sam. 11:2–25) was explained by distinguishing between what David had done in his office as king, in which he had been a man after God's own heart (cp. 1 Sam. 13:14) and what he had done as a private individual, which was not to be excused.

Such justifications for moral difficulties had begun to come under attack at the end of the seventeenth century, for example in Pierre Bayle's *Dictionnaire historique et critique* (1697) and Deist writers in England in the seventeenth and eighteenth centuries had drawn attention to moral difficulties in the Bible as part of their advocacy of a purified form of Christianity based upon reason. These attacks had come from outside the church circles that defended the Bible as divine revelation. As the nineteenth century progressed the moral crudities in the Bible became increasingly problematic for scholarly circles *within* the churches. This led to a different approach to the ethical teaching contained in the Bible, which saw it not so much as divine legislation as immature human moral understanding. This, again, was not entirely new. Writers such as Aquinas, who believed in natural law, believed that universal moral principles could be discerned by the use of human reason and that what was discerned was ultimately divinely given. In the case of the legislative and ethical material contained in the Old Testament, this was a specific application of the principles of natural law to the special circumstances of ancient Israel. This special application had been revealed by God through figures such as Moses. The change that came about, in Britain at any rate, in the nineteenth century, was that it was no longer believed that God had revealed to ancient

Israel specific applications of natural law. Rather, the ethical and legislative material in the Old Testament represented the human understanding of morality of a people that had yet to make a good deal of progress towards a mature appreciation of what was right and wrong.

What was basically at issue was the understanding of the nature of God. Joshua 10:40 not only stated that Joshua had utterly destroyed the Canaanites; it said that he had done this in obedience to God. Traditional orthodoxy said that this was because of the idolatry and wickedness of the Canaanites, but the question had to be asked whether utter destruction was an appropriate punishment; whether there might have been innocent women and children among those destroyed. After all, Abraham had raised a similar point with God, according to Genesis 18:25. Another passage that raised problems was Genesis 22:2, God's command to Abraham to sacrifice his son Isaac. How, it was asked, could someone honestly believe that God was commanding him to do something that was so obviously immoral? As long as people accepted that what God commanded could only always be right, there was no problem. As soon as people began to expect at least the highest moral insights from God (and compare Gen. 18:25 again: "shall not the judge of all the earth do what is right?") a different explanation had to be found for Genesis 22:2. It was found in the view that Abraham must have had both a defective idea of God and of the moral status of his son (Mozley, 1896: 57). After all, in Roman society the idea of *patria potestas* (the power of the father) gave far-reaching powers to a father over his children.

The upshot of all this is that the Old Testament came to be seen not as a revelation of God but as a *record* of his revelation. It was a *record* of the way in which God had educated the human race and ancient Israel in particular, leading them from belief in many gods to belief in one God, from crude superstitions to higher moral principles. This meant that Joshua 10:40 did *not* teach that it was God who had commanded Joshua to destroy the Canaanites utterly. Joshua, or the biblical author/editor, may have thought this, but if so this was a mistake, a mistake due to an inadequate understanding of the nature of God and the value of human lives.

Another impulse behind this new approach to the ethical material in the Old and New Testament was that in the late-eighteenth and nineteenth centuries the traditional link between the Old and New Testaments had been severed, in the sense that the Old Testament was no longer seen principally as a collection of prophecies and "types" which had their fulfilment in Christ. The Old Testament was read in its historical setting as a witness to the faith of ancient Israel. But in one regard the link between the testaments was not severed. The New Testament provided the moral touchstone by which the ethical content of the Old Testament was to be judged. The fact that Jesus had commanded his followers to love their enemies (Matt. 5:44) meant that passages such as Joshua 10:40 or Psalm 139:21 ("do not I hate them that hate thee, O Lord?") could not be taken seriously as revealing the nature of God. At best they indicated the immature and inadequate ideas of God and morality possessed by the Old Testament writers.

The view that the Old Testament is the record of the progressive self-revelation of God, or the record of the divine education of the Israelites/ the human race, has lost the attraction that it exercised so powerfully in the nineteenth and first part of the twentieth century (see Rogerson, 1982). This is because it was based upon an understanding of the course of ancient Israel's history that has been superseded. It has become clear, for example, that Joshua did not invade the land of Canaan and utterly destroy its inhabitants, as claimed in the book of Joshua. Rather, the occupation of the land was a peaceful process engaged in by ethnic groups other than, but also including, proto-Israelites in the early Iron Age. The stories in Joshua *may* record internal battles in the land of Canaan between proto-Israelites and their neighbours. The *rhetoric* of the stories, utter destruction of enemies, does not represent reality, but accords with the conventions of the *descriptions* of war in the ancient Near East. This does not make them any more acceptable from the moral point of view, but it does undermine any attempt to date parts of the Old Testament in such a way as to produce an evolutionistic account of the alleged moral progress of the Israelites from crude to less crude stages. Similarly, the story of Abraham's "sacrifice" of Isaac in Genesis 22 cannot be regarded as coming from an "early" part of the Bible which indicates a time when child sacrifice was acceptable to Israelites. It is probably a "late" passage that contains many literary and theological subtleties.

However, if the idea of progressive revelation or progressive education is out of favour, the phenomena that it was meant to account for still remain and have to be faced up to. These phenomena are moral teachings in the New as well as the Old Testament that fall short not only of the standard implied in the teaching of Jesus, but the actual legislation of many modern societies. Examples from the Old Testament would be the death penalty for offences such as striking or cursing one's parents (Exod. 21:15, 17) and adultery (Deut. 22:22) not to mention homicide (Gen. 9:6). A New Testament example would be the statement in 1 Timothy 2:12 that no woman is to have any authority over men, or is to be allowed to teach them, although it must be acknowledged that within conservative evangelical circles today there are those who oppose the ordination of women because they believe that passages such as 1 Timothy 2:12 teach male "headship" over women.

As earlier chapters and sections in this book have shown, the churches have never maintained that Christians must obey all the prescriptions in the Old Testament. Various ways of squaring the apparent circle, that God revealed his law in the Old Testament but that much of this is not binding, have been reviewed. What finally broke down, at least in scholarly critical circles in the nineteenth and twentieth centuries, was the belief that moral prescriptions in the Old Testament had been revealed by God. This happened for number of reasons, including the abandonment of the belief that God had dictated the Bible to the inspired authors who were responsible for it. Just as the growth of the biblical traditions to their present form was seen as a human process that in some of its stages could be traced by literary criticism, so the growth of the legislative and moral parts of the Old Testament could be partly traced and understood in the wider context of the laws of the neighbours of ancient Israel. The discovery in 1901–1902 of the laws of Hammurabi, some of which closely paralleled the laws of Exodus 21–22 contributed to this new understanding. However, abandonment of the belief that biblical injunctions had been revealed by God does not mean that this material in the Bible has lost all theological or ethical significance. On the contrary, abandonment of older "mechanical" theories of the origin of the Bible has made way for new approaches which arguably enable its ethical material to be appreciated to a greater extent than was previously possible.

Chapter 9

A New Approach: Example not Precept

The main thesis of what now follows is that the Bible does not so much provide us with precepts, that is, specific commands, but rather with examples that we can follow. It is not being suggested that the Bible contains *no* binding moral precepts; obviously, it does, and a case in point would be its prohibition of murder. However, the thrust of what is being maintained here is that while many of the Bible's precepts cannot be applied directly to today's world for reasons that will be explained shortly, a process of moral discernment and action within them can be recognized. Such discernment and action can then become an example and challenge to modern users of the Bible.

This is described in the heading above as a new approach, yet in some ways it is not so new. Already in the writings of Paul there is the principle that the written code kills but the Spirit gives life (2 Cor. 3:4), a principle taken up and developed by Augustine (see above, p. 36). Indeed, there can also be found in Paul a tendency to sum up the biblical law and commandments in principles that call for creative moral thinking and action rather than strict obedience to a written code. In Romans 13:8–10 Paul writes: "Owe no one anything, except to love one another; for he who loves his neighbour has fulfilled the law. The commandments, 'You shall not commit adultery, You shall not kill, You shall not steal, You shall not covet,' and any other commandment, are summed up in this sentence, 'You shall love your neighbour as yourself.' Love does no wrong to a neighbour; therefore love is the fulfilling of the law."

It might well be objected that this is far too vague; that "love" can be defined in many ways and that the outcome can be sloppy and flabby. There is also the difficulty of deciding what it means to love one's neighbour as oneself. Does this imply that one begins from a self-interested love, one in which the standards of one's own comfort and enjoyment are paramount? A plausible answer to this question could be that Paul is quoting from Leviticus 19:18: you shall love your neighbour as yourself, and that he has clearly defined the nature and behaviour of love in 1 Corinthians 13:4–7. It is noteworthy that the definitions of love in 1 Corinthians 13 are partly in terms of negatives, which means that the definitions are not prescriptive, but are invitations to creative and imaginative action. The same, incidentally, is true of the Parable of the Good Samaritan in Luke 10:30–37. Asked to give a legal ruling on the meaning of neighbour, Jesus tells a story and says, "Go and do thou likewise," which is an invitation to imaginative and creative action. Some examples of how this can work in using the Bible will now be given.

1. *Deuteronomy 15:12–18*

This passage is the equivalent in Deuteronomy of the laws in Exodus 21:2–11, and some preliminary observations can be made. First, it is often pointed out that it is significant that the first main block of laws in the Old Testament (in Exod. 21) begins with laws limiting slavery. This is unique in the ancient world as far as we know, and makes a theological statement about the kind of people God expects to have to serve him. While slavery may have been an inevitable consequence of economic conditions in ancient Israel, it is not allowed to become a permanent condition unless a slave voluntarily gives up his freedom in a publicly-witnessed ceremony (Exod. 21:5–6). The theological point is that slavery is to be no permanent and dominating feature of the people of God, a people delivered by God from slavery in Egypt. The second point is that while the law allows slavery, it implicitly condemns it by limiting it, a point that is even more obvious in Deuteronomy 15. Thus we can say that the *spirit* of this law is against slavery and it was this spirit that was enacted when slavery was finally outlawed in Britain in the eighteenth and nineteenth centuries. The *letter* of the law had, of course, been used to justify slavery.

In turning to Deuteronomy 15:12–18, the first point to notice is the gloss in verse 12, which grants the same rights to a female slave as to a male slave. In Exodus 21:7–11 it is explicitly stated that a female slave does *not* have the same rights as a male slave ("she shall not go out [i.e., become free] as the male slaves do"). Only if a female slave marries her master or his son does she have any hope of freedom, for example, if she is divorced by her husband. The granting to the female slave of the same rights as the male slave in Deuteronomy 15 is an instance of a developing moral sensitivity in the Old Testament that extends justice and compassion to groups previously excluded.

The second point is the language, in verses 13–14, that commands the master to furnish the freed slave liberally (literally, the Hebrew means "bejewel") out of his flock, his threshing floor and his wine press. This injunction recognizes that freedom without economic support may condemn the freed slave to a speedy return to slavery. The master has a responsibility to ensure that this does not happen. Yet no precise figures of sheep or measures of grain and wine are given. Instead, an appeal is made to the conscience and imaginative creativity of the master: "as the LORD your God has blessed you, you shall give to him" (v. 14). This is what I have called elsewhere a "structure of grace" – a social and administrative arrangement designed to allow graciousness and compassion to function in human relationships. It is a response to what comes in verse 15, which is what I call an "imperative of redemption" – a command based upon the fact that the person commanded has experienced and is enjoying redemption, a situation that calls for a response conditioned by the fact of redemption, "You shall remember that you were a slave in the land of Egypt, and the LORD your God redeemed you; therefore I command you this today." A literalist approach to this passage can make no use of it, unless it has the highly dubious aim of supporting slavery! It certainly cannot be applied to readers who own neither slaves nor sheep nor threshing floors nor vineyards. Seen, however, as an example of creating a "structure of grace" in response to an "imperative of redemption" it can challenge modern readers to ask what "imperatives of redemption" might be applicable to modern circumstances of enslavement, and what "structures of grace" might be created in those circumstances.

2. Exodus 23:9–12

This is another passage which, because it is addressed to a slave-owning agricultural society, can hardly be applied literally to modern urban situations. Its spiritual dynamics are, however, challenging. The section begins with an "imperative of redemption" – a call not to oppress a "stranger" (Hebrew, *ger;* probably meaning an Israelite or foreigner alienated from, and therefore not living with, his kinsfolk) because the Israelites were once "strangers" in the land of Egypt. The point of contact is the vulnerability of the stranger having to live separated from kinsfolk, and the vulnerability of the Israelites enslaved in Egypt. Verses 10–11 command a seventh-year rest for Israelite lands, vineyards and olive orchards. This is not an agricultural necessity turned into a theological virtue. Israelite "fields" (cultivated areas) had to be fallowed every other year, while there was no such necessity for vineyards and olive orchards. What we have is a statement that the land and its various forms of produce are not to be used for the sole benefit of those lucky enough to possess these things. The produce is regularly (every seventh year) to be given over to the poor and to the wild beasts. In this way, owners of fields and orchards are reminded of their need for solidarity with the poor, and also with wild animals, even if some of the latter were permitted to be hunted for food.

Verse 12 is a version of the Sabbath day commandment that gives as the reason for the cessation of work the need to allow those domesticated animals to rest that provided the main pulling and carrying power in ancient Israelite agriculture. After the ox and the ass is a mention of the servants and the alien (Hebrew, *ger*). The effect of the passage is to accord to animals and servants a right to be able to rest. A master has no right to exploit his working animals and his servants. They must be treated with respect. The passage is another example of commandments whose value is in the challenge they make to modern readers to consider how respect for the environment and for animals and people who might be exploited, can be given practical expression by means of appropriate "structures of grace."

3. *Leviticus 25*

This is a famous passage which has made prominent the idea of the Jubilee, the word being derived from the Hebrew, *yovel,* for the trumpet that is blown to herald the arrival of the forty-ninth or fiftieth year. It begins in verses 3–7 with a statement of the rule of the Sabbath year, similar to that found in Exodus 23:10–11, with the slight difference that in the seventh year vineyards are not to be pruned. What is produced by unsown fields and unpruned vineyards may be consumed by the Israelites and their slaves and cattle, but the land and the vineyards are to be allowed to rest. This is the prelude to the seven times seven sabbatical year, the jubilee year. It is not clear whether this is the forty-ninth year (i.e., the seventh of the series of seven sabbatical years) or the fiftieth year (which would presumably imply that there were two consecutive sabbatical years – v. 11 used the term fiftieth year) but this question is not important in the present context.

In the jubilee year (whether the forty-ninth or fiftieth year) each person shall return to his property, which means that all the economic factors which have led to some people losing their property (e.g., through debt) and others gaining it, will be cancelled out by all property owners returning to their own land. This process is not unmindful of the potential unfairnesses that might occur, and verses 25–27 outline a situation in which a man who has been forced to sell his property to someone outside his family later becomes sufficiently prosperous to be able to buy it back. In such a case the original owner is expected to pay a fair price when he returns to his land at the jubilee. Only if the original owner remains too poor to buy back his land does he receive it back free of charge at the jubilee. In the case of dwelling houses a distinction is made between those in walled cities and those in unwalled villages. The jubilee law applies only to the latter. Other provisions in the chapter forbid the charging of interest to fellow-Israelites and do not allow Israelites to enslave each other (v. 39; on the assumption that "brother" means fellow Israelite and not a member of the extended family).

The question has often been raised whether the jubilee was ever observed or enforced; whether, for example, the rules in verses 26–27 about a man who has become prosperous being required to pay a fair price for his property reflect experience of actual cases, of whether they are the outcome of theoretical debates. The matter is not of concern here. Even if the jubilee laws were never enforced they articulate an ideal which is a challenge to all societies. They recognize that economic factors affect relationships between people, making some poorer and others richer, and forcing some into dependence upon others. This state of affairs is not acceptable among a people redeemed by God. The distortions of social relationships do not reflect his will. It is therefore necessary for there to be periodic readjustments so that all relationships are put back on an equal footing and the malign consequences of economic processes can be negated.

In spite of the high profile jubilee campaign before and up to the year 2000 whose aim was to get the debts of developing countries cancelled – a point not addressed in Leviticus 25 but derived from Deuteronomy 15:1–6 – the provisions of Leviticus 25 cannot be applied to the urban and landowning situation of modern Europe and North America. Yet as the jubilee campaign indicated, even if not based upon Leviticus 25, the biblical text can present challenges to the modern world to formulate "structures of grace" appropriate to its conditions. The particular principle enunciated in Leviticus 25 is that people are more important than economic processes and that the latter should not be allowed to force people into poverty, slavery and dependence. This is a message that has increasing relevance in a global economy that is still unable to deal with the desperate poverty of millions in Africa, where, in the so-called developed world, there are unacceptably high levels of unemployment with all the social ills that unemployment generates.

4. *1 Corinthians 8 and 10:14–33*

The question of whether or not to eat food offered to idols is not one that is likely to trouble readers of the Bible, at any rate in the so-called developed world. The matter is yet another example of the vast cultural difference between the world of the Bible and that of the modern world. Yet, arguably, Paul's discussion of the question as it related to the congregation in Corinth offers valuable insights as to how ethical matters can be tackled in a Christian context.

The basic problem was that if people were going to eat meat in the Hellenistic/Roman world they were most likely to obtain it from pagan temples where it had been offered in sacrifice but was surplus to the requirements of the rite, the priests or the offerers. What should be the attitude of Christians to the purchase and consumption of such meat, or other food items that could be obtained from a temple? (For a full discussion of these passages, see Barrett, 1968: 183–245). The particular problem with meat is that it is unlikely that it would have been killed so as to drain the blood. This would be especially problematic for observant Jews, but also for Christians if we assume that the Apostolic Decrees in Acts 15:23–29 had actually been formulated and circulated to churches. The theological question was whether the household consumption of temple food implied belief in the gods to whom it had been offered, or whether it was rendered impure because it had been used in rites connected with these gods.

The remarkable thing about Paul's response is that he seems to lay down only one principle, which is that one should not offend the conscience of a fellow Christian (1 Cor. 8:9–13). What this means in practice is that a person's behaviour should be guided by the impact that it may have on others. Left to himself, Paul seems to be saying that since other gods do not exist (1 Cor. 8:4) and everything belongs to God and the Father of Jesus Christ (1 Cor. 8:6; 10:26), there is no good reason not to eat meat or food obtained from a temple. However, life is not lived on an isolated, individual level. Paul came into contact with Christians and non-Christians, and his guiding principle in such cases was that his behaviour should not be a stumbling block to others, a stumbling block that either threatened the faith of a Christian or put obstacles in the way of a non-Christian coming to faith. Thus at 1 Corinthians 8:9 Paul warns his readers against using their liberty to eat whatever they want in such a way that it becomes a stumbling block to the weak, for example, Christians who are not fully persuaded that idols do not exist. In 1 Corinthians 10:27–29 Paul discusses the situation in which a Christian is invited to a meal by a non-Christian.

His advice is to eat anything that is provided and only to raise an objection if the non-Christian explicitly mentions that the food has been offered in sacrifice.

What we see in Paul's advice is the spirit and not the letter. Here is no rigid application of rules but action that is appropriate to the situation. If there is a rule implied it is, as stated above, that one's behaviour should not be a stumbling block to others. Formulated in Christian terms it means doing everything for the sake of the gospel (cp. 1 Cor. 9:23). What is being advocated is not an unprincipled way of life tailored entirely to pleasing other people and gaining their approval. The operative word is "gospel" and Paul had very clear ideas about what this was and what it implied, and indeed devoted much space in his letters to attacking what he considered to be distortions or misunderstandings of the gospel. But it was because he had such a clear idea of what the gospel was, and what was important and what was not, that he could "become all things to all men" (1 Cor. 9:22). What he meant by this is that he could go a long way to agreeing with others, even with those of quite different persuasions, on matters that were not essential to the gospel. His originality lay in being able to discern what mattered from what was not essential, and in being able to disengage his emotions and actions from the need to engage in or uphold what was not essential. Put in terms of what has been formulated earlier in this chapter, he took as an "imperative of redemption" the principle that what he did should be for the sake of the gospel, and he created "structures of grace" appropriate to the people with whom he was dealing.

Chapter 10

Case Studies

When all has been said and done, it is case studies that ultimately disclose the persuasiveness or otherwise of any attempt to use the Bible in social and moral questions. To conclude the present work three areas will be addressed in the hope that the matters discussed will be put into perspective, and guidance will be provided for readers as to how they might use the Bible if they wish to do so. The areas will be marriage, divorce and remarriage, the charging of interest, and human sexuality.

1. *Marriage, Divorce and Remarriage*

The Bible contains very little on the subject of marriage, and certainly does not offer a definition. There are, of course, a few stories about events that lead up to marriages. Examples that come readily to mind include the journey of Abraham's servant to the city of his master's brother Nahor to seek a wife for Isaac in Genesis 24 or the encounters between Ruth and Boaz in the book of Ruth. In the story of Jacob, Jacob serves his uncle Laban for seven years in order to marry, as he expects, Laban's younger daughter Rachel, only to discover that he has been given the elder daughter Leah. He serves for a further seven years in order to obtain Rachel (Gen. 29:15–30). The legislation in Deuteronomy 22:13–20 defends a newly-married woman whose husband accuses her of not being a virgin, although she is to be put to death by stoning if the allegation proves to be true. Even the New Testament takes it for granted that readers will be familiar with the marriage customs that are implicit in the parable of the wise and foolish virgins (Matt. 25:1–13). The parable implies that there is a festive procession in which the bride is conducted from her father's house to that of her husband. Deuteronomy 22:23–29 indicates that betrothal confers on a woman the same legal status and obligations as marriage, such that if a man rapes a betrothed woman he commits an offence punishable by death, but if he rapes an unbetrothed woman he is liable to a fine, is required to marry the woman and may not subsequently divorce her.

If the Bible is reticent about marriage, it is also reticent about divorce. Divorce is referred to only in Deuteronomy 24:1–4 and possibly in Malachi 2:14–16 in the Old Testament. In the New Testament it is mentioned at Matthew 5:31–32 (paralleled in Luke 16:18) and 19:3–9, Mark 10:2–13 and 1 Corinthians 7:10–15. The passage in Deuteronomy is the only one that says anything about the grounds or mechanism of divorce, and then only by way of comment on the main point, which is that a divorced woman who had remarried and then had either been widowed or divorced again may not remarry her first husband. It should be noted that the passage in Deuteronomy seems to accept that there is no problem with the divorced woman remarrying. The incidental information that is given is that divorce is effected by the husband writing a bill of divorce, giving it into the hand of the woman and sending her out of the house. It would be interesting to know whether any modern literalists would take the view that this is a procedure that still has validity. Malachi 2:14–16 also mentions divorce only incidentally. The passage seems to imply situations in which men are being unfaithful to the wife of their youth, presumably by divorcing them with a view to marrying a younger woman, or by simply taking a second, younger, wife who will supplant the older wife. The passage concludes with the statement that "he hates divorce" for which the ancient Greek version had "I [God] hate divorce" which is followed by many modern translations. Perhaps the most important feature of the passage is that marriage is described as a covenant (Mal. 2:14). Isaiah 50:1 contains the phrase "your mother's bill of divorce with which I put her away" but this adds nothing to our knowledge.

The background to the New Testament passages is that by the first century CE it had become general practice not to put to death a woman who had committed adultery but to regard the offence as a ground for divorce. Many readers will understandably object that John 7:53–8:11 records an incident in which Jesus delivers a woman taken in adultery from death by stoning, by challenging his audience to produce one person who is without sin, who will cast the first stone, a challenge that is not taken up. The difficulty is that this passage is not found in any of the most ancient witnesses to the Greek text of John, and that in some manuscripts is it is placed after John 7:36 or John 21:25 or Luke 21:38, with some variations of text. It is impossible to know how ancient the story is or whether it accurately reflected Jewish practice of the period. The same is true of Jewish discussions around the beginning of the Common Era regarding whether adulteresses should be stoned or strangled. It is difficult to know whether they were merely discussions, or whether they reflected actual practice. John 18:31 states that the Jews (under Roman occupation) were not permitted to put anyone to death, and this certainly seems to be the implication of the account of the death of Jesus in the gospels. A development in Jewish law and practice was that rules were drawn up about the proper form of bills of divorce and how they were to be served on the women to be affected. It is clear that these rules were designed to make divorce procedures as difficult as possible, and that they were thus designed to give some protection to women.

In Mark 10:2–12, Jesus is asked by the Pharisees whether divorce is lawful. As so often in these stories, Jesus replies by way of a question, "What did Moses command?" They allude to Deuteronomy 24:1, to which Jesus replies that Moses was taking account of human hardness of heart. The ideal is stated in Genesis 1:27 and 2:24, that a man and a woman become "one flesh" in marriage, and that human activity should not put asunder what God has joined together. Verses 10–12 record what Jesus then said in private to the disciples, that a man who divorces and remarries commits adultery against his divorced wife, and that a divorced woman who remarries commits adultery against her former husband. Matthew 19:3–9 substantially repeats this but adds the significant phrase "except for unchastity"; that is, Matthew appears to say that a man who divorces his wife and remarries does *not* commit adultery if he divorced his wife because of her unchastity (Greek, *porneia* – a word usually translated by "fornication," i.e., sexual intercourse outside marriage and equivalent to adultery in this context). Matthew 5:32 repeats this declaration. "Every one who divorces his wife, except on the ground of unchastity, (*porneia*) makes her an adulteress."

Paul, in 1 Corinthians 7:10–16, gives advice on marriage and divorce. When he says, "not I but the Lord" he is presumably referring to tradition that is believed to come from Jesus. This teaching is that a man should not divorce his wife, and that a wife should not separate from her husband. If she does separate from him, she must remain single or seek to be reconciled to her husband. In verse 12, Paul deals on his own authority with the problem of a Christian woman who has a non–Christian husband. The advice is that the couple should stay together if the husband wishes that they should. Only if he desires them to separate should the woman consider herself to be no longer bound.

In what follows, an attempt will be made to sketch briefly the history of the understanding of these passages and how this has affected practice in different churches. The section will conclude with a discussion of the issues raised by the passage and their use.

Readers in Britain, but not necessarily in North America and certainly not on the continent of Europe, will be familiar with people being married in church, that is, with the situation that a church service conducted by an accredited Minister of Religion serves the dual function of being both a civil ceremony recognized by the state, and a religious occasion on which vows are taken in the name of God. The fact that people can also be married at a non-religious ceremony performed by a civil registrar is often seen in Britain as a secular deviation from the norm, which is that of marriages conducted wholly in a church building. In fact it took over a thousand years for the Church in the west to absorb marriage, so to speak, so that it became something essentially religious and Christian, something reckoned as a sacrament, at least in (Roman) Catholic practice (see Brink, 1982: 330–36).

As the Church expanded in the Roman Empire, it did so in a realm in which marriage and divorce were governed by civil laws and customs. The Church had no direct control over these and could only affect the behaviour of its members through pastoral discipline such as requiring members to do penance if their marital practices were deemed to be sinful. There was no unanimity on the question of divorce and remarriage. Although a majority opinion was increasingly that marriage was indissoluble from a Christian point of view (cp. Mark 10:9, "what... God has joined together, let not man put asunder") an impressive list of Church Fathers could be assembled who, while not favouring divorce and remarriage, nonetheless held that a marriage could be ended by the adultery of one partner and that the innocent party could remarry (see Phillips, 1988: 37). It was not until the Council of Lyon in 1274 that marriage was declared to be one of the seven sacraments, with the consequence that Christian marriage could only be solemnized in church and by a priest. However, the Council of Lyon only confirmed and officially stated, developments that had been taking place during the preceding centuries.

The official declaration of the sacramental nature and therefore indissolubility of marriage also brought the need for provisions to deal with marriage breakdown and irregularities. This was done by allowing marriages to be annulled or for spouses to be allowed to separate. In the latter case they remained married and could not remarry. In the former case a duly authorized person (e.g., the Pope) or body declared that the marriage had been deficient and had not, in effect, taken place. A ground for annulment that could be, and which was often, advanced was that it had taken place within degrees of kin relationship prohibited in the Bible. A case in point would be Henry VIII's marriage to Catherine of Aragon. Catherine had formerly been the wife of Henry's elder brother Arthur. After Arthur's death a dispensation from the Pope allowed Henry to marry Catherine, a relationship explicitly forbidden by Leviticus 18:16 ("you shall not uncover the nakedness of your brother's wife"). Henry believed that the failure of this union to produce a male heir was divine punishment for disobeying the biblical injunction and therefore sought an annulment. Phillips (1988: 74) notes that one of the arguments used by Catherine's supporters (who opposed the annulment) was that Deuteronomy 25:5–10 provided biblical justification for the union of Henry and Catherine. This law states that it is the duty of the brother of a man who dies childless (which was the case with Arthur) to marry the widow and to raise up children in the name of the deceased. Henry's supporters argued that this law had been abrogated by the coming of Christ. Legislation, which in effect made the Church of England independent from Rome, enabled a convention to declare in 1533 that the marriage to Catherine had been unlawful and that it was null and void.

It is perhaps one of the accidents of history that the *Reformatio Legum*, which would have provided the Anglican Church and England with "a more liberal divorce policy than any European church or country" (Phillips, 1988: 84) and which was proposed in the 1550s was never given legal effect. The Anglican Church maintained the Catholic view that marriage was indissoluble. This was not the opinion of the main continental reformers, nor of some of the leading English reformers.

Both Luther and Calvin allowed divorced for adultery and desertion, with the possibility that the innocent party could remarry. However, divorces were not to be granted lightly, nor was adultery to be allowed to become an easy way of ending a marriage. Other reformers had similar views, and were even prepared to extend the list of misdemeanours that might allow a marriage to be ended (Phillips, 1988: 63). Tyndale, who was strongly influenced by the Continental reformers, also allowed a husband to divorce an adulterous wife and to remarry. If a husband deserted his wife he should be banished once a year had passed, and the woman should be free to remarry (Phillips, 1988: 78). Archbishop Cranmer was asked to report on the case of the Marquis of Northampton, who had gained a separation from his wife on the grounds of adultery in 1542 and who remarried in 1548 claiming that this action was in accordance with the Word of God (Phillips, 1988: 80). Cranmer's report upheld the Marquis' action, appealing to Matthew 19:9 and arguing that since in marriage two people become "one flesh," that union is broken by adultery, thus dissolving the marriage. Cranmer also argued that if Paul allowed divorce in cases where a non-Christian separated from a Christian, adultery was a more serious offence and therefore also a ground for divorce (Phillips, 1988: 79–80).

In the event, and despite views such as those expressed by Tyndale and Cranmer, the Church of England became committed to the view of the indissolubility of marriage, a view that has prevailed to the present time, in spite of attempts from the 1970s onwards to devise schemes to allow innocent divorced persons to remarry in church. An official guide to the marriage law issued to clergy of the Church of England in 1992 explains that while clergy may not legally be prevented from solemnizing the marriage in church of a person or persons who have been granted a civil divorce, the Convocation of Canterbury expressed the view in 1957 that "the Church should not allow the use of the Marriage Service in such cases" (Anglican Marriage, 1992: 27). The same publication notes that the Church in Wales holds that a marriage that has been ended by divorce in a civil court still exists in canon law, and that it cannot therefore solemnize the marriage of a divorced person whose ex-spouse is still living (Anglican Marriage, 1992: 28).

One of the interesting things about the position traditionally adopted by the Church of England is the fact that it ignored the teaching of Jesus and Paul, as understood both by many of the early Fathers as well as by all the major reformers. While rejecting the authority and some doctrines of the Roman Catholic Church it nevertheless adhered to the view of marriage and divorce that had developed in western Catholic tradition. It asserted that there were only two sacraments (Baptism and Holy Communion) yet continued to accord to marriage the status and mystique of a sacrament. The advent of biblical criticism, something viewed with suspicion and received only reluctantly by the Church of England, curiously gave support to its view of the indissolubility of marriage.

An example of this can be found in the commentary on Mark by A. E. J. Rawlinson, published in 1925. Rawlinson would later become Bishop of Derby. His commentary is a fine piece of work, distinguished by its knowledge of German biblical criticism and by its theological sensitivity. The section on Mark 10:2–12 implicitly makes much of the view almost universally accepted in non-Roman Catholic scholarship at the time, that Mark was the first of the Synoptic Gospels (Matthew, Mark and Luke) to have been written, and that Matthew and Luke used Mark as a primary source. If one had to choose between Mark and Matthew as sources for the teaching of Jesus on the subject of divorce, it was clear that Mark was to be preferred. In describing what Mark 10:2–12 was about, Rawlinson assumed that Jesus took a more rigorous attitude to divorce that either of the two well-known contemporary Pharisaic schools, those of Hillel and Shammai. That of Shammai was the more rigorous, holding that divorce was permitted only on the ground of adultery. According to Rawlinson, Jesus was asked for an opinion on the matter because he was known to have strongly-held views (Rawlinson, 1927: 134). After getting his questioners to refer back to the ruling of Moses in Deuteronomy 24:1–3, Jesus appealed to the opening chapters of Genesis, from which he deduced "the ideal of permanent and indissoluble marriage." The version of the incident in Matthew 19:3–12 contained interpolated glosses (i.e., those saying "except for fornication") and had the effect of modifying "the sense of our Lord's words as to represent Him as having merely taken sides in a current rabbinical dispute" (Rawlinson, 1927: 135). In a long footnote Rawlinson rejected the view of German and British scholars who admitted that the exceptive clauses were interpolations, but held that they correctly interpreted what Jesus had said. He noted that the Eastern churches followed Matthew's gospel and allowed divorce on the ground of adultery. However, "the Canon Law of the Western Church recognised in certain circumstances divorce *a mensa et toro* [i.e., separation from bed and board], but never divorce *a vinculo matrimonii* [i.e., divorce from the marriage bond] with liberty of remarriage." Thus Rawlinson was able to adduce biblical and dominical authority for the traditional western (Catholic) view of the indissolubility of marriage.

Rawlinson finds an ally (at least as far as exegesis goes) in the commentary on Matthew by the Swiss Protestant scholar Ulrich Luz (Luz, 1997: 97–99). Luz believes that the Matthean community upheld the essential "once-for-allness" of marriage, and that the provision that a man could put away his adulterous wife was not a provision for divorce but for separation, with no possibility that the husband could remarry. The position of the Matthean community was therefore more rigorous than that of the school of Shammai, which did allow the remarriage of the aggrieved husband. If, as an exegete, Luz believes that the "Catholic" understanding of Matthew 19 and related texts is justified, he goes on to argue that this interpretation is not helpful in today's world and that one needs to set the divorce prohibition in the context of the New Testament as a whole. He also feels uneasy about approaching marriage as a distinctively Christian institution in an open and secular society.

Luz is writing a commentary on Matthew and not a handbook on practical theology so he can be forgiven for not going into details on this matter in what is in fact an outstanding commentary. In what follows now an attempt will be made to use the biblical passages to address the situations that exist in western society today (for which see above all Giddens, 1992).

As a starting point let it be assumed that Mark 10:2–9 faithfully records the teaching of Jesus and that the additions in Matthew regarding adultery were intended to allow separation in such cases, but not divorce and remarriage. The crucial question then becomes the intention of Jesus in referring back to Genesis 1:27 and 2:24, and to the statement that Moses gave the commandment about divorce because of human hardness of heart. Was Jesus legislating, and saying that marriage should never be ended ("what God has joined together, let not man put asunder") under any circumstances, or was he articulating an ideal, an ideal of which many would fall short? If the first alternative is accepted, it has to be said that even the most rigorous Christian position has not adhered to it, given that ways have been found of annulling marriages, even while upholding their indissolubility. The second alternative offers a way of accepting the passage fully while applying it sensitively to pastoral situations.

The Markan passage states the ideal that marriage is life long. This is a fine ideal and one that is to be commended and upheld in every possible way. However, the human beings who contract marriages are fallible creatures living in an as-yet unredeemed world. What is the attitude of the Christian gospel to be to those whose marriages break down? To use the teaching of Jesus to say, in effect, that such people have committed an almost unforgivable sin is surely to misunderstand what the mission and message of Jesus are about. Worshippers who use forms of service that regularly employ prayers of confession of sin followed by the pronouncement of absolution do not, if they are sincere, suppose that they are capable of living perfect lives. They hope in the mercy of God for that divine acceptance that will alone help them to become what God wishes them to be. Why should it be any different in the case of people whose marriages have failed? Of course, there is a balance to be struck here. The divine mercy can be abused so as to produce the charge that sin is multiplied so that grace can abound (cp. Rom. 6:1). Pastoral practice that gave the impression that marital breakdown was a trivial matter and that the church would solemnize as many marriages as an individual wanted, would be a travesty of what was needed. People whose marriages have failed have fallen short of an ideal – but then so have those who have failed in their love of God and of their neighbour, and there is no suggestion that such people should be excluded in any way from the ministrations of the churches. There is the further point that the Christian gospel is about the mercy of

God making it possible for people to face the future with new hope. It has to be asked why people whose marriages have failed, who have sincerely repented and who wish to make a new start with another partner, should not be able to do so in the presence of God and with the prayers, full support and blessing of the Church. In short, it is possible to accept and uphold the ideals expressed in Mark 10:2–9 and at the same time to act compassionately and in accordance with the gospel in cases where there is failure to maintain the ideals. What is called for is neither a legalistic and rigourist approach, on the one hand, nor an "anything goes" approach on the other. The gospel demands that we ask the question "how is the gospel proclaimed and furthered in this particular case?" and that action follows from the answer. In practice it will mean that in some cases it will seem right to solemnize fully in church the marriage of a divorced person or persons. In other cases it will be felt that such a step would not be appropriate, although this would not rule out the giving of such blessing and pastoral support as would further the gospel.

2. *Interest*

For most of the history of the Church it has been believed that that the Bible taught that it was wrong to charge interest on loans. The standard laws in the Old Testament relevant to the matter were as follows:

1. Exodus 22:25, "If you lend money to any of my people with you who is poor, you shall not be to him as a creditor, and you shall not exact interest from him."
2. Leviticus 25:35–37, "And if your brother becomes poor...take no interest from him or increase. You shall not lend him your money at interest, nor give him your food for profit."
3. Deuteronomy 23:20, "To a foreigner [Hebrew, *nokhri*] you may lend upon interest, but to your brother you shall not lend upon interest."

Laws are, of course, one thing; their observance and enforcement is another matter. Nehemiah 5:1–13 records that Nehemiah accused the nobles and officials in late fifth-century Judah of exacting interest from fellow Jews (Neh. 5:7), and that he ordered them to return to their owners the properties and produce that had been appropriated by the money-lenders when interest payments had not been met. That interest was in fact charged by Israelites to other Israelites is indicated by the fact that those who refused to do this were regarded as god-fearing. Psalm15 lists the qualities demanded of those who wish to dwell on God's holy hill, and includes in the list "who does not put out his money at interest." In Ezekiel 18:8, 13 and 17 where there are catalogues of good and bad behaviour, not lending on interest is a mark of good behaviour, doing so is a sign of bad behaviour.

The Old Testament, then, allowed interest to be charged to non-Israelites, but forbade charging it to fellow Israelites. Particularly significant for Christian attitudes was the teaching of Jesus, and especially Luke 6:34–35: "And if you lend to those from whom you hope to receive, what credit is that to you? Even sinners lend to sinners, to receive as much again; But love your enemies, and do good, and lend, expecting nothing in return." Whatever may have been intended by these words, they were taken to mean that Jesus had explicitly forbidden the charging of interest. There is, of course, a parable in the New Testament that implies, in the words of Driver and Miles (1952: I, 175) the lawfulness of charging interest in the case of commercial loans, namely the parable of the Talents (Matt. 25:14–30; cp. v. 27, "you ought to have invested my money with the bankers"). However, according to Gertz (2004: 674) it is clear from the parable that the Master is foreign and not Jewish. Whether or not this is accurate, the fact is that the New Testament was understood in the early Church to forbid the charging of interest on loans.

From the fourth to the fourteenth centuries, Councils of the Church forbade the charging of interest (see Sprandel, 2004: 682). The Council of Elvira (305 CE) forbade usury to clergy and laity (Canon XX in Jonkers, 1954: 10). The Council of Arles (314 CE) prescribed excommunication for clergy who practised usury (Jonkers, 1954: 26) while the Council of Nicaea (325 CE), in condemning usury appealed to Psalm 15:5 (Jonkers, 1954: 45). The Second and Third Lateran Councils (1139 and 1179 CE) resolved to deny Christian burial to money-lenders, who were likened to Jews, Moslems, soldiers and homosexuals (Sprandel, 2004: 682). The Council of Lyon (1274 CE) threatened with excommunication any priest who gave the sacraments to money-lenders, while the Council of Vienna (1311 CE) condemned as a heresy the view that usury was not a sin. The influence of the philosophy of Aristotle upon theology from the twelfth century strengthened the anti-usury view. Aristotle (cp. *The Nicomachean Ethics* 5.9–10, in Rackham, 1934: 283) held that money was a "middle term" [Greek, *meson*] that enabled different commodities to be valued with a view to their fair and equitable exchange. Money did not exist "by nature" (*Ethics* 5.11, Rackham: 285) and therefore could not grow or increase by interest being charged upon it. Calvin would later pour scorn upon this argument.

The expansion of trade from the fifteenth century in Europe made the exchange of credit necessary, as it was dangerous to take large sums of money from one place to another. Banks were set up in trading countries (e.g., Italy and England) that would facilitate the exchange of credit, and the charging of interest began to be justified on the grounds of the risks involved in making loans (see generally Parks, 2005). In 1462 the Franciscans established credit institutions that did not charge interest but levied a handling charge. This is apparently also modern Moslem banking practice, given that the *Qur'an* expressly forbids the charging of interest (*Qur'an*, Sura 2.279). The Franciscan method was recognized as legitimate by the Fifth Lateran Council in 1515 (Sprandel, 2004: 684).

At the Reformation, Luther upheld the traditional view that interest should not be charged (see O'Donovan and O'Donovan, 1999: 602–608). Calvin took the opposite view (in his *Letters of Advice*, see O'Donovan and O'Donovan, 1999: 682–84). "There is no scriptural passage that totally bans all usury," he declared and he rejected the interpretation of Luke 6:34–35 that saw it as teaching of Jesus directed again usury. It was, instead, a command to help the poor, even if this meant not being repaid. Calvin regarded the argument that money could not naturally engender money (Aristotle's view, also stated by Ambrose and Chrysostom) as frivolous. He pointed out that one could lawfully make money by renting out a piece of ground. If this was so, why was it unlawful to make money by loaning it? He concluded that usury should not be judged "according to a few passages of Scripture, but in accordance with the principle of equity" (O'Donovan and O'Donovan, 1999: 683). Calvin's view was generally followed in reformed Protestantism (see Markham, 2004: 689–70) and was even used as anti-Roman Catholic polemic, the Catholics being accused of wanting to control trade in Christian countries by forbidding interest. In Catholic circles meanwhile, the view was gaining ground that what should be prohibited was not the charging of interest as such, but the charging of excessive interest. In 1872 the Vatican agreed that interest of up to eight percent was not excessive. On the other hand, William Temple (Temple, 1942: 116), who held that banks should be publicly administered institutions, argued that where credit was lent by a book-keeping entry, the only ethically-defensible charge was the cost of administration, of no more than half or two-thirds percent.

The matter of interest indicates the perils of applying biblical injunctions to changing situations in a crude literalist fashion. That this is not just a modern problem is shown by Calvin's attitude to the matter. He was quite unwilling to let "a few passages of scripture" interfere with the economic realities of his day, and he was ready to challenge traditional interpretation of the Bible, such as that Jesus had explicitly forbidden usury. By saying that the whole subject should be governed by equity, he was laying down a sound principle for the use of the Bible. Baxter's view (*Directory*, 2000: 116), that usury was evil only if it was against justice and charity, was also a sound insight. The whole tenor of the Old Testament is that the exploitation of the poor and needy is an offence against God, (cp. Exod. 22:21–24) and the Old Testament had numerous devices for trying to neutralize the effects of exploitation, for example, the Sabbath day of rest, the sabbatical year, the periodic cancellation of loans, the restriction of slavery to six years, and the jubilee year. Further, it sought to engender a "brother-ethic" in which it was the duty of any Israelite to assist a fellow Israelite who had fallen into poverty. Today's world, with its cashless societies, credit cards, mortgages, and at the same time crushing poverty in parts of Africa can hardly be addressed by "a few passages of scripture" addressed to totally different economic and social situations. At the same time, all that the Bible has to say about justice and equity as between individuals and nations is sufficient to enable a Christian social ethic to be articulated in a world in which the charging of interest has led to the most appalling distortions of the relation between rich and poor nations, and between people within those nations.

3. *Human Sexuality*

In 1998 the Lambeth Conference of bishops of the worldwide Anglican Communion voted overwhelmingly for a resolution that stated that homosexuality was contrary to the teaching of the Bible. This resolution has had, and continues to have, serious implications for the unity of the Anglican Communion and for individuals within it whose sexual orientation is that they are attracted to members of the same sex. The resolution raises two fundamental questions. Does the Bible teach that homosexuality is wrong? Secondly, assuming that it does so, what should the Churches make of this teaching, given that they have been prepared to accept that clear biblical teaching on the death penalty for capital offences, or on not charging interest on loans, is no longer relevant in today's world?

The main passages that have traditionally been appealed to are as follows. (a) Genesis 19, which is the story of the two angels coming to visit Lot in the city of Sodom. He grants them hospitality, only for "the men of the city...both young and old, all the people to the last man" (Gen. 19:4) to surround the house and to demand that the men (i.e., the angels) be brought out to them, "that we may know them" (Gen. 19:5). That the verb "know" is being used in the sense of "have sexual intercourse with" is made clear by Lot's reply, that he has two virgin daughters whom he would be pleased to make available so that the mob could "do to them as you please" (Gen. 19:8). In the event this is not necessary because the angels smite with blindness the mob that is pressing against the door. The incident has given rise to the word "sodomy" in English, so named, according to the *New Penguin English Dictionary* "from the homosexual desires of the men of Sodom/Genesis 19:1–11."

The difficulty with this passage is that it proves too much and raises the kind of question that an Origen might have puzzled over (see below, p. 30). The texts says that "all the people to the last man" surrounded Lot's house, and if it is to be assumed that they were all desirous of having sexual relations with Lot's male (angelic) visitors one wonders what normal daily life was like in the city, or why it was that Lot chose to reside there. The fact is that, for whatever reasons, the city of Sodom acquired a symbolic significance in the Bible as the epitome of an evil city (Gen. 13:13), and that its evil and destruction were often used as bywords (cp. Isa. 1:9–10; Ezek. 16:48–49). Whatever may have been the origins of the story in Genesis 19, the narrative was fashioned in order to demonstrate the extreme wickedness of the whole male population by representing their wickedness as male sexual lust. That the passage regards a public male sexual orgy as something very wicked is clear, and presumably most, if not all, readers of this book will agree that public sexual orgies are undesirable, to put the matter mildly. The problem is that what Genesis 19 condemns is a far cry from what English law allows, which is homosexual acts committed in private by consenting male adults aged 16 or over. Whatever one may think of this law, it is difficult to see how Genesis 19 can be applicable to it.

(b) Leviticus 18:22, "You shall not lie with a male as with a woman; it is an abomination" and Leviticus 20:13, "If a man lies with a male as with a woman both of them have committed an abomination; they shall be put to death, their blood is upon them."

It is to be noted that these passages occur in the context of general prohibitions of sexual relations between close relatives, and that in Leviticus 20 the death penalty is prescribed for some of the cases of intercourse between close relatives. The cases mentioned include a man's intercourse with his father's wife (a wife additional to his own mother), his daughter-in-law, and his wife's mother. The penalty of being "cut off," that is, by the death penalty, is prescribed for a man who has intercourse with his stepsister, his maternal or paternal aunt, and his uncle's wife or his brother's wife. The same penalty is required for a man who has intercourse with a woman (presumably his wife) during her menstrual periods.

It is to be noted that the condemnation of homosexual activity occurs in the context of the condemnation of a series of *heterosexual* irregularities. If one if going to be accurate about what the Bible teaches (leaving aside *how* that teaching should be applied) it ought to be pointed out that many heterosexual relationships and practices are condemned in Leviticus 18 and 20, otherwise the false impression may be given that homosexual relationships are especially singled out. They are not. It is also the case that the passages assume that irregularities within *polygamous* families are being condemned. It has been conjectured that the purpose of the passages is to restrict endogamous marriages (i.e., marriages within the close kin group) so as not to endanger the begetting of children who will ensure the continuance of the social unit. Homosexual liaisons are condemned, according to this view, because they will not produce children. It is interesting to note that both Abraham and Jacob are recorded as having relationships expressly forbidden in Leviticus 18 and 20. According to Genesis 20:12, Sarah was Abraham's stepsister (forbidden in Lev. 20:17) while Jacob married two sisters (Gen. 29:15–30, forbidden in Lev. 18:18).

(c) Romans 1:27, "men...gave up natural relations with women and were consumed with passion for one another, men committing shameless acts with men and receiving in their own persons the due penalty for their error." This verse occurs in the context of a passage in which corrupt behaviour is condemned, the point being that human beings have a sense of right and wrong given to them by God, which they have ignored. Among the things condemned are envy, murder, strife, deceit, malignity, gossip, slander, insolence, haughtiness, boasting, disobedience to parents, foolishness, faithlessness, heartlessness and ruthlessness.

(d) 1 Corinthians 6:9–10, "Do not be deceived, neither the immoral, nor idolaters, nor adulterers, nor sexual perverts, nor thieves, nor the greedy, nor drunkards, nor revilers, nor robbers will inherit the Kingdom of God." The translation "sexual perverts" covers two Greek words that are rendered by the Revised Version as "effeminate" and "abusers of themselves with men." Homosexual practices are obviously referred to.

(e) 1 Timothy 1:9–10, "the law is not laid down for the just but for the lawless and disobedient, for the ungodly and sinners, for the unholy and profane, for murderers of fathers and murderers of mothers, for manslayers, immoral persons [RV, fornicators], sodomites [RV, abusers of themselves with men], kidnappers, liars, perjurers, and whatever else is contrary to sound doctrine." Before these passages are commented on, it should be noted that the Bible arguably describes without condemnation one homosexual relationship, namely that between David and Jonathan. When Jonathan first meets David we are told that "the soul of Jonathan was knit to the soul of David, and Jonathan loved him as his own soul" (1 Sam. 18:1). As an expression of this relationship Jonathan made a covenant with David and gave him his robe, his armour, his sword, his bow and his girdle (1 Sam. 18:4). When David learns the news of Jonathan's death he exclaims, "I am distressed for you, my brother Jonathan; very pleasant have you been to me; your love to me was wonderful, passing the love of women" (2 Sam. 1:26).

As a general comment on the passages (a) to (e) it should be observed that the references to homosexual acts (except for Gen. 19) occur in contexts that list many other types of unacceptable behaviour. This, of course, does not explain away the references to homosexual acts, but does raise questions about how the biblical passages are to be understood and applied. The statement in 1 Corinthians 6:9–10 is a case in point. When it says that adulterers will not inherit the Kingdom of God, does it allow no possibility of repentance? If the verses are taken literally they will imply that the heir to the British throne and his wife, whose marriage was blessed by the Church of England, will not inherit the Kingdom of God, however we understand this latter phrase. It could be argued that if repentance on the part of adulterers will make inheritance of the Kingdom of God possible, the same ought to be true of "abusers of themselves with men," yet a man who had once had a homosexual relationship but who was now living a celibate life was recently debarred from becoming a bishop in the Church of England because of his earlier homosexual relationship. It is difficult to escape the conclusion that in using the Bible in the debate about homosexuality, those who argue that the Bible condemns it pluck texts from their context and ignore the implications of clear biblical teaching on other matters which occur along with the references to homosexual acts.

In seeking to deal positively with the matter the following points will be made: (1) the Bible condemns certain homosexual and heterosexual acts but not the orientations; (2) the best biblical principle for dealing with the matter is that implied in Paul's discussion about whether a [Corinthian] Christian should eat food offered to idols.

1. It has been pointed out above that with the exception of Genesis 19, which condemns a public homosexual orgy, the other passages which mention homosexual acts all occur in verses which condemn certain heterosexual acts as well as non-sexual misdemeanours such as murder and theft. Nowhere in these passages does the Bible condemn the tendency or orientation that underlies these actions, otherwise we should have to

reckon with categories of people, for example, murderers, thieves, adulterers, whose orientations were an irreversible part of their humanity. The Bible is concerned to condemn *actions*, and to hold open the possibility of repentance and forgiveness where such actions are contrary to God's will. To argue that an exception should be made in the case of people who commit homosexual acts is to indulge in special pleading.

It is often argued that attention should be paid to Genesis 2:24, "Therefore a man leaves his father and his mother and cleaves to his wife, and they become one flesh." This verse has been said to prescribe the divine intention for sexual relationships in terms of "one man, one woman, for life." The "for life" element is not unreasonably deduced from the use made of the passage by Jesus at Mark 10:9 ("what God has joined together..."). There are several difficulties with this argument. The first is that Old Testament society was polygamous, as is indicated not only by passages such as Leviticus 18 and 20, but by the fact that Jacob, Elkanah, David and Solomon, to name the most obvious cases, had more than one wife at the same time, without earning any condemnation in the Bible. If Genesis 2:24 prescribed heterosexual monogamy, this was unknown to, or ignored by the editors/compilers of the narratives concerning the characters just named. The second difficulty is that the text implies that the man leaves his own family and joins that of his wife. This is certainly how the text was understood by some commentators in the nineteenth century, who saw in it a hint that ancient semitic marriage had once been matri-local (i.e., a man became, on marriage, a member of his wife's kin group). The third difficulty is that understanding the passage as a categorical rule (i.e., one applying in any circumstances) involves adopting the view that what is commanded in the Bible necessarily rules out any alternative. It is true that some Reformers took this approach, and earned the scorn of people such as Baxter (see above, p. 68) who argued that if these people were right, then the Lord's Supper should be administered to eleven or twelve men only, in an upper room at evening time.

2. Let it be assumed that what has just been written has established that the Bible condemns a number of heterosexual acts and certain homosexual acts. Let it also be added that within both types of relationships there can be abuses that are not mentioned in the Bible, but which many people would regard as unacceptable. These would include physical abuse such as one partner regularly physically attacking other, or mental abuse in which one partner refused to speak to the other for long periods, or inflicted pain by means of cutting remarks, sarcasm, or a refusal to forget past failings or mistakes. The point that is being made here is that it is a gross misuse of the

Bible to conclude from its teaching that homosexuality is wrong, with the implication that heterosexuality is in order. The fact is that the Bible condemns a number of *heterosexual* practices, and if the further points made above are taken into consideration, there may be heterosexual relationships that outwardly look in order (e.g., a man and woman who have been married for many years) but which inwardly are characterized by physical or mental abuse. Such relationships would surely fail the test of loving one's neighbour as oneself. What the Bible condemns is not the *nature* of a relationship (i.e., whether it is homosexual or heterosexual) but what is done *within* the relationship, and it is at this point that the story of David and Jonathan becomes important. This is a relationship about which the word "love" is used unashamedly (cp. 2 Sam. 1:26 – Hebrew, *ahavah*). It is characterized by the kind of generosity through which love finds outward expressions, as in Jonathan giving to David his own robe, armour and weapons (1 Sam. 18:4). It is also a relationship that is characterized by loyalty, as when Jonathan warns David that it will be dangerous for him to attend a new-moon feast hosted by Saul (1 Sam. 20:1–42). It might be objected to this example that David and Jonathan did not *live* together, but such an argument only points to the need for profound analysis when sexual relationships are being considered. It has to be asked why it would be more acceptable for a man and a woman to live together as husband and wife in a relationship that left much to be desired from the point of view of mutual love and understanding, than for two women or two men to live together in a relationship that was a profound expression of mutual trust and support.

If, from a biblical point of view, a principle is to be found that will help make decisions about dealing with same-sex partnerships, the best candidate will be that enunciated by Paul in 1 Corinthians 9:12, that we should "endure everything rather than put an obstacle in the way of the gospel of Christ." In practice, this will mean that the scales are weighted against Christians in same-sex relationships and they will be targeted by those in the churches who believe that the Bible forbids same-sex relationships as well as those outside the churches who find such relationships "unnatural." On the positive side, this approach removes the charge that people in same-sex relationships are doing something that is abominable to God. How they *conduct* their lives together will be something to which they will be answerable to God – but that will also be true of those in heterosexual relationships.

There is no reason why, if the gospel of Christ is not hindered, same-sex partners should not be active members of churches, in either lay or ordained roles. This will not at present be possible in parts of the world, or parts of countries such as Britain and North America, where there are strong aversions to same-sex partnerships, but it is surprising how attitudes are changing, even in Christian circles. Forty years ago it would have been a scandal if a man and woman had been living in the same house without being married. Today, it is not unknown for unmarried and committed evangelical Christian students of opposite sexes to be living under the same roof without any awareness that they are doing anything wrong or unusual. It can be confidently predicted that in forty years' time same-sex partnerships will not be regarded as wrong or unusual, even in many Church circles.

Conclusion

A lot of ground has been covered in this book since it began with an inquirer trying to "go by the book." Hopefully, the rather tortuous journey will not have been a waste of time or effort. The purpose of this conclusion is not to give definite answers to issues that have been raised but to set out parameters within which answers may be sought. Readers can seek their own answers. The argument will proceed by a series of propositions, which are not necessarily logically connected.

1. In order to use the Bible responsibly it is necessary to be aware of its whole content and of the fact that many of its presuppositions, for example, the death penalty for adultery, are considered to be immoral in modern western societies. The question must be answered how a text with immoral demands can provide resources for modern Christian living.

2. In order to use the Bible responsibly it is necessary to acknowledge that in the course of history the churches have changed their position on various issues, in response to changing economic and social pressures. Examples would be usury, which the churches condemned for over a thousand years, slavery, which the church tolerated for even longer, and issues such as marriage with the sister of a man's deceased wife, which the Church of England regarded as forbidden by the laws of God in Scripture until the 1940s. The implications of these changes in attitude must be considered carefully.

3. In order to use the Bible responsibly it is necessary to acknowledge that many leading Christian thinkers, such as Augustine, Aquinas and Luther

have held that if Old Testament laws have binding power upon Christians, this is not because they are in the Bible but because they are expressions of universal natural law. When Old Testament passages are quoted in moral debates as though they do have binding power because they are in the Bible, it needs to be asked why a powerful stream of Christian tradition has held otherwise.

4. In order to use the Bible responsibly it is necessary to acknowledge that anyone who appeals to the Bible does so *selectively*. This is as true of "Bible-believing Christians" as anyone else (and see point 1 above). It is important for those who use the Bible to be able to justify *why* they use it selectively and why, for example, they might insist that the Bible condemns homosexual acts, but does not require Christians to eat kosher meat (see Acts 15:28–29).

5. In order to use the Bible responsibly it is necessary to acknowledge that on certain issues, theologians whose commitment to the Bible cannot be called into question, have nonetheless taken different stands. A case in point is the issue of divorce and remarriage. Reformers such as Luther, Calvin and Tyndale took the Bible to allow divorce on the ground of adultery, with the possibility that an innocent party could remarry. Such a view would be rejected by many conservative Evangelicals today.

6. The use of the Bible has traditionally been guided by certain theological principles, such as that the letter kills but the spirit gives life (cp. 2 Cor. 3:6) or that the Bible's main function is to express the gospel and not be to be used as a law book. When any issue is being addressed in the light of the Bible's teaching it must be asked what theological principles are being invoked or implied.

7. Any responsible use of the Bible must acknowledge that it comes from a culture completely different from that of modern western society. It must be acknowledged that ancient Israelite society as portrayed in the Bible was polygamous, and that many of its laws assumed that landowners possessed slaves, vineyards, and olive orchards. Further, it must be acknowledged that the Bible says nothing about many modern problems, such as nuclear war, abortion or euthanasia. This does not mean that the Bible cannot be used to address modern issues. It does mean that its use calls for a high degree of knowledge, discernment, theological acumen, understanding of

human nature and society, and the belief that against all the odds, the Bible can bring light and hope into a world still darkened by so much ignorance and inhumanity.

BIBLIOGRAPHY

Anglican Marriage in England and Wales. 1992. *A Guide to the Law for Clergy.* London: The Faculty Office of the Archbishop of Canterbury.

Aquinas. 1915. *The Summa Theologica of St. Thomas Aquinas.* Part II (First Part) (QQXC–CXIV); London: Burns Oates & Washbourne.

Aristotle. 1956. *The Nicomachean Ethics.* Ed. H. Rackham. The Loeb Classical Library; London/Cambridge, MA: William Heinemann/Harvard University Press.

Augustine. 1958. *Aurelii Augustini Opera 5, Corpus Christianorum.* Series Latina, 33; Turnholt: Brepols.

Barrett, C. K., 1968. *The First Epistle to the Corinthians.* Black's New Testament Commentaries; London: Adam & Charles Black.

Baxter, R., 2000. *The Practical Works of Richard Baxter.* I. *A Christian Directory.* Morgan, PA: Soli Deo Gloria Publications.

Bornkamm, H., 1948. *Luther und das Alte Testament.* Tübingen: J. C. B. Mohr (Paul Siebeck).

— *Luther in Mid-Career 1521–1530.* London: Darton, Longman & Todd.

Braulik, G. 1986. *Deuteronium 1-16, 17.* Die neue Echter Bibel; Würzburg: Echter Verlag.

Brink, L., 1982. "Ehe/Eherecht/Ehescheidung VI." *Theologische Realenzyklopädie* 9: 330–36. Berlin: W. de Gruyter.

Burger, J. D. 1951. *Augustine: L'esprit et la lettre = De spiritu et littera, texte, intro., traduction et notes.* Neuchâtel: Messeiller.

Calvin, J., 1964. *Calvin Opera, Corpus Reformatorum.* Volume 24 (1882); Reprint New York & London/Frankfurt am Main: Johnson Reprint/Minerva 1964.

— n.d. *Institutes of the Christian Religion.* Florida: Macdonald Publishing.

Clementine Homilies. n.d. *The Apostolical Constitutions.* Ante-Nicene Christian Library, 17; Edinburgh, T&T Clark.

Coleman, P. 1980. *Christian Attitudes to Homosexuality.* London: SPCK.

Collinson, P. 1967. *The Elizabethan Puritan Movement.* London: Jonathan Cape.

Crouzel, H. 1982. "Ehe/Eherecht/Ehescheidung V." *Theologische Realenzyklopädie* 9: 325-30. Berlin: W. de Gruyter.

Driver, G. R., and J. C. Miles. 1952. *The Babylonian Laws.* Oxford: Clarendon Press.

Fischer, J. A. 1993. *Die Apostolischen Väter.* Schriften des Urchristentums, I; Darmstadt: Wissenschaftliche Buchgesellschaft.

Gertz, J. C. 2004. "Zins II." *Theologische Realenzyklopädie* 36: 672-74. Berlin: W. de Gruyter.

Giddens, A. 1992. *The Transformation of Intimacy: Sexuality, Love and Eroticism in Modern Societies.* Cambridge: Polity Press.

Grudem, W. 1994. *Systematic Theology: An Introduction to Biblical Doctrine.* Leicester: Inter-Varsity Press.

Hooker, R. 1975. *Of the Laws of Ecclesiastical Polity, an Abridged Edition.* Ed. A. S. McGrade, B. Vickers; London: Sidgwick & Jackson.

Ibn Ezra, Abraham. 1976. *Perushe HaTorah.* Jerusalem: Mossad Harav Kook.

Jonkers, E. J. 1954. *Acta et Symbola Conciliorum quae Saeculo Quarto habita sunt.* Textus Minores, 19; Leiden: E. J. Brill.

Kapach, J. D. 1972. *Moshe ben Maimun: Moreh HaNebukhim/Dalalat elHairin.* Jerusalem: Mossad Harav Kook.

Kerrigan, A. 1952. *St. Cyril of Alexandria: Interpreter of the Old Testament.* Rome: Pontificio Istituto Biblico.

Klein, R. 2000. "Sklaverei IV." *Theologische Realenzyklopädie* 31: 379-83. Berlin: W. de Gruyter.

Körtner, U. H. J., and M. Leutzsch. 1998. *Papiasfragmente: Hirt des Hermas.* Schriften des Urchristentums, III; Darmstadt: Wissenschaftliche Buchgesellschaft.

Luther, M. 1904. *Eine Unterrichtung, wie sich die Christen in Mosen sollen schicken in Werke.* Kritischer Gesamtausgabe, 16; Weimar: Bölaus.

Luther, M. 1962. *Luther's Works, Volume 45: The Christian in Society.* Philadelphia: Muhlenberg Press.

Luz, U. 1985-2002. *Das Evangelium nach Matthäus.* Evangelisch-Katholischer Kommentar zum Neuen Testament 1/3; Zürich/Neukirchen: Benziger Verlag/Neukirchener Verlag.

MacCulloch, D. 2003. *Reformation: Europe's House Divided 1490–1700.* London: Allen Lane, 2003.

Maier, J. 1985. *The Temple Scroll: An Introduction, Translation & Commentary.* Trans. R. T. White; JOSTSup, 34; Sheffield: JSOT Press; German original 1978. *Die Tempelrolle vom Toten Meer.* Munich: Ernst Reinhardt Verlag.

Markham, I. 2004. "Zins V." *Theologische Realenzyklopädie* 36: 687–91. Berlin: W. de Gruyter.

Melammed, E. Z. 1990. " 'Observe' and 'Remember' Spoken in One Utterance." In *The Ten Commandments in History and Tradition,* ed. B.-Z. Segal: 191-217. Jerusalem: The Magnes Press.

Metzger, M. (ed.). 1985, 1986. *Les Constitutions Apostoliques,* I (livres I–II); II (livres III–VI). Sources Chrétiennes 320 and 329; Paris: Les Éditions de Cerf.

Michaelis, J. D. 1814. *Commentaries on the Laws of Moses.* Trans. A. Smith. 4 vols.; London.

Mozley, J. B. 1896, new edition. *Ruling Ideas in Early Ages and their Relation to the Old Testament.* London: Longmans, Green 1896.

Nowak, D. 1974. *Law and Theology in Judaism.* New York: Ktav Publishing House.

O'Donovan, O., and J. L. O'Donovan, eds. 1999. *From Irenaeus to Grotius: A Sourcebook in Christian Political Thought.* Grand Rapids: Eerdmans.

Origen. *Homélies sur L'Exode.* 1985. Ed. Marcel Borret. Sources Chrétiennes, 321; Paris: Les Éditions de Cerf.

Parker, T. H. L. 1986. *Calvin's Old Testament Commentaries.* Edinburgh: T&T Clark.

Parks, T. 2005. *Medici Money: Banking, Metaphysics and Art in Fifteenth-Century Florence*. London: Profile Books.

Phillips, R. 1988. *Putting Asunder: A History of Divorce in Western Society*. Cambridge: Cambridge University Press.

Pines, S. 1963. *Moses Maimonides: The Guide of the Perplexed*. Chicago and London: University of Chicago Press.

Rawlinson, A. E. J. 1927, 2nd edn. *St. Mark, with Introduction, Commentary and Additional Notes*. Westminster Commentaries; London: Methuen.

Rogerson, J. W. 1982. "Progressive Revelation: Its History and its Value as a Key to Old Testament Interpretation." The A. S. Peake Memorial Lecture 1981. *Epworth Review* 9: 73–86.

Rordorf, W., and A. Tuilier. 1978. *La Doctrine des douze apôtres (Didaché): Introduction, texte, traduction, notes, appendice et index*. Sources Chrétiennes, 248; Paris: Les Éditions de Cerf.

Rordorf, W. 1999, 4th edn. "Didache." In *Religion in Geschichte und Gegenwart*: II, 836. Tübingen: Mohr Siebeck.

Rosenbaum, M., and A. M. Silberman. 1946. *Pentateuch with Targum Onkelos, Haphtaroth and Prayers for the Sabbath and Rashi's Commentary*. London: Shapiro, Valentine.

Safrai, S., and M. Stern. 1974. *The Jewish People in the First Century: Historical Geography, Political History, Social, Cultural and Religious Life and Institutions*. Compendia Rerum Iudaicarum ad Novum Testamentum, Section One; Assen: Van Gorcum.

Schild, M. E. 1982. "Ehe/Eherecht/Ehescheidung VII." *Theologische Realenzyklopädie* 9: 336–46. Berlin: W. de Gruyter.

Smend, R., and U. Luz. 1981. *Gesetz*. Biblische Konfrontationen; Stuttgart: Verlag W. Kohlhammer.

Sprandel, R. 2004. "Zins IV." *Theologische Realenzyklopädie* 36: 681–87. Berlin: W. de Gruyter.

Temple, W. 1942. *Christianity and Social Order*. Harmondsworth: Penguin.

Tertullien. 1994. *Contre Marcion Livre III*. Ed. René Braun. Sources Chrétiennes, 399; Paris: Les Éditions de Cerf.

Urbach, E. E. 1975. *The Sages: Their Concepts and Beliefs*. Trans. I. Abrahams. Jerusalem: Magnes Press. Hebrew original, *Hazal. Pirqe Emunoth weDeoth*. Jerusalem: Magnes Press, 1971.

Wengst, K. ed. 1984. *Didache (Apostellehre), Barnabasbrief, Zweiter Klemensbrief, Schrift an Diognet*. Schriften des Urchristentums, II; Darmstadt: Wissenschaftliche Buchgesellschaft.

White, L. 1967. "The Historic Roots of our Ecologic Crisis." *Science* 155: 1203–207.

INDEX

INDEX OF REFERENCES

OLD TESTAMENT

APOCRYPHA

NEW TESTAMENT

EARLY CHRISTIAN WRITINGS

Index of Names and Subjects